THE GODDESS,
MOTHER OF THE TRINITY

A Jungian Implication

THE GODDESS, MOTHER OF THE TRINITY

MOTHER OF THE TRINITY

A Jungian Implication

THE GODDESS, MOTHER OF THE TRINITY

A Jungian Implication

John P. Dourley

Studies in the Psychology of Religion
Volume 4

The Edwin Mellen Press
Lewiston/Queenston/Lampeter

Library of Congress Cataloging-in-Publication Data

Dourley, John P.
   The Goddess, Mother of the Trinity : a Jungian implication / John
P. Dourley.
     p.   cm. -- (Studies in the psychology of religion ; v. 4)
   Includes bibliographical references and index.
   ISBN 0-88946-244-5
   1. Psychoanalysis and religion. 2. Jung, C. G. (Carl Gustav),
1875-1961. 3. Trinity--Psychological aspects. 4. Goddesses.
5. Eckhart, Meister, d. 1327. I. Title. II. Series.
BF175.4.R44D68 1990
200'.1'9--dc20   90-37579
                                         CIP

This is volume 4 in the continuing series
Studies in the Psychology of Religion
Volume 4 ISBN 0-88946-244-5
SPR Series ISBN 0-88946-247-X

A CIP catalog record for this book
is available from the British Library.

The Edwin Mellen Press   The Edwin Mellen Press
Box 450   Box 67
Lewiston, New York   Queenston, Ontario
USA 14092   CANADA L0S 1L0

The Edwin Mellen Press, Ltd.
Lampeter, Dyfed, Wales
UNITED KINGDOM SA48 7DY

Printed in the United States of America

TABLE OF CONTENTS

CHAPTER ONE

JUNG'S CRITIQUE OF BIBLICAL IMAGINATION:
AN APPRECIATIVE UNDERMINING

At the heart of Jung's response to Christianity, taken organically and in the context of his whole work, lies an ambivalence best described as an appreciative undermining. This appreciative undermining is radical. For, when fully appropriated it graciously dissolves certain foundational features of the Christian myth and its tradition, both ecclesial and theological. The spirit of this appreciative undermining is not, by and large, aggressive, nor acerbic, though it is insistent. At the same time it is not occasional or peripheral to the substance of Jung's psychology. On the contrary, it is woven into its very fabric. In fact, this undermining element is foundational to both the counter myth within Jung's psychology and to the metaphysical and theological import which this counter myth bears within itself. Thus, focusing on the appreciative undermining of Christianity at the heart of Jung's mythology becomes a process of making explicit the ontological and epistemological implications, with their weighty consequence for the understanding of religion and Christianity, contained in the substance of his psychology. The full import of these unforced ramifications of Jung's thought are only now becoming evident in the widespread current endeavour to render fully conscious the deeper religious and philosophical implications of his psychology.[1] This work hopes to contribute to that effort.

Jung's appreciative undermining of the biblical imagination informing not only mainstream orthodox Christianity, but, by extension, all forms of transcendental monotheism, must be evenly addressed. If it is approached responsibly, both of the apparently contradictory facets which make it up must be honoured. Thus, to deny that Jung's psychology is authentically appreciative of Christianity would be as great a falsification as the counter denial that the vision and empathy his psychology embodies is ultimately broader and deeper than the Christian and so, in the final analysis, works to undermine it by surpassing it.

Because he was born into the Christian tradition, Jung's psychology is more consistently engaged, both appreciatively and critically, with Christianity than other religions. This is not to deny that Jung came to appreciate all religions, living and dead, as treasured expressions of their common source, the collective unconscious. It is to affirm that he was personally driven by his initially negative experience of Christianity and by his own psycho-religious experience to a prolonged engagement with Christianity. This engagement led him to an extensive examination of other religions, prodded by the question of why his own tradition could not respond to his own religious experience and to the spirituality this experience fostered in him. Finally, this search led Jung to his mature hypothesis of the psycho-genesis of religion through the inter-play of consciousness with its numinous ground and creator in a process whose teleology was toward a wholeness that Christianity could with difficulty currently foster.

The dialectic involved in Jung's appreciation and criticism of Christianity is a distillation of a lifetime of effort and seeking. The subtlety

---

1.   *Cf.* as a sampling Edward F. Edinger, *The Creation of Consciousness: Jung's Myth for Modern Man* (Toronto: Inner City, 1984), *The Bible and the Psyche: Individuation Symbolism in the Old Testament* (Toronto: Inner City, 1986); Clifford A. Brown, *Jung's Hermeneutic of Doctrine* (Chicago: Scholar's Press, 1981); Murray Stein, *Jung's Treatment of Christianity: The Psychotherapy of a Religious Tradition* (Willmette: Chiron, 1985); John P. Dourley, *The Psyche as Sacrament: A Comparative Study of C. G. Jung and Paul Tillich* (Toronto: Inner City, 1981), *The Illness That We Are: a Jungian Critique of Christianity* (Toronto: Inner City, 1984), *Love, Celibacy and the Inner Marriage* (Toronto: Inner City, 1987).

implied in his appreciative undermining of the tradition into which he was born frequently appears throughout his writings in precise formulations of which the following is typical:

> It is therefore well to examine carefully the psychological aspects of the individuation process in the light of Christian tradition, which can describe it for us with an exactitude and impressiveness far surpassing our feeble attempts, even though the Christian image of the self - Christ - lacks the shadow that properly belongs to it.[2]

In this typical passage Jung both appreciates the myth developed around the Christ image and accuses it of bearing a now pathologizing one-sidedness.

In spite of his difficulties with the tradition in his youth typified in the depression it induced in his minister father,[3] Jung in his maturity viewed Christianity as the still presiding myth in Western culture. As such, it continued to provide the West with its culture hero, the Christ figure, and with many of the values operative in its cultural ethos.[4] Thus Jung remained appreciative of the revelation or compensation toward the spiritual which occasioned Christianity's genesis, met the aspirations of the society into which it came, and even into his day continued to provide it with the sacralization required by all societies as their cohesive principle.

At the same time, Jung remained equally aware that the Christian myth could, in his day and ours, less easily meet the demands of psycho-spiritual maturation felt by ever increasing numbers within both the Christian community and the wider culture. In the elaboration of his own psychology, myth, and metaphysics, Jung clearly identified those features of the Christian myth which increasingly disqualified it as a bearer of spiritual and psychological maturity and life to its supposed societal and cultural

---

2.   C. G. Jung, "Christ, a Symbol of the Self," *Aion*, CW 9ii, par. 79, p. 45. The same point is made in *ibid.*, par. 74, p. 41, and pars. 76-79, pp. 42-45. All citations from the *Collected Works* (Princeton: Princeton University Press, 1957-1979) will contain title, volume number, paragraph, and page.

3.   *Cf.* Jung's references to the faith-induced pathology of his father in *Memories. Dreams, Reflections*, ed. Aniela Jaffe, trans. Richard and Clara Winston (New York: Random House, 1961), pp. 42f, 52, 53 and 73.

4.   C. G. Jung, "Christ, A Symbol of the Self," *Aion*, CW 9ii, par. 69, p. 36.

4

constituencies. Three major features of the pathologizing potential of the still presiding myth Jung identified as externalism, which would encompass all forms of supernaturalism, literalism and historicism.

Perhaps the most disabling of these features is the first, for it may be the core of the pathology carried by the latter two. Externalism refers to the "systematic blindness"[5] that Jung attributed to the theological conviction that God was somehow beyond the psyche, or in his terms, "*outside* man."[6] Once the sense of inorganic transcendence such an imagination implies is established, then God's incursions into the psyche from beyond it in his revealing and saving endeavours can be taken literally and, as in the Christian tradition, even dated, as the basis of an "historical religion." Such consciousness and its attendant imagination divest the soul of the experience of its native divinity through the projection of God beyond the soul. As this self-divestiture becomes a residual form of consciousness, the psyche grows progressively insensitive, sometimes to the point of immunity, to the power of its own archetypal and symbolic expression as contained in sacred literature which itself emanates from the depths of the human soul. In this manner even their own so-called revelation becomes a body of foreign truths to the believers' minds it is alleged to enliven with God's word or "Good News."

So also does literalism, the inevitable companion of such externalism, diminish or destroy the religious impulse in humanity, paradoxically, in its misguided effort to preserve the "objectivity" of the revelation it unwittingly renders incredible. Jung captures the religiously debilitating effects of literalism when he writes of the fascination of the fundamentalist mind with the historical miracles of Christ, a fascination which deprives its holder of the spiritual meaning of the miraculous accounts. He writes:

> The spirit and meaning of Christ are present and perceptible to us even without the aid of miracles. Miracles appeal only to the understanding of those who cannot perceive the meaning. They are mere substitutes for the not understood reality of the spirit.[7]

C. G. Jung, "Psychology and Religion," CW 11, par. 100, p. 58.

6. *Ibid.*

7. C. G. Jung, "The Answer to Job," CW 11, par. 554, p. 360.

Among others, Paul Tillich frequently pointed to the tragic diminishment of the religious impulse and its humanizing potential accompanying modernity's loss of the symbolic sense. Tillich would try to dramatize this loss by pointing to the attenuated sense of the sacred, of religion and of religious discourse betrayed by the phrase, "only a symbol."[8] On the lips of the fundamentalist the phrase, for Tillich, pointed to that consciousness capable of understanding the meaning of mythic or symbolic discourse only when it was divested of its spiritual import, reduced to literalism and given a so called "historical" basis. For Tillich the tragedy of a consciousness unable to appreciate symbolic address pointed to a deeper tragedy, namely the severance of consciousness, which he attributes originally to Aquinas,[9] from a sense of its inner connectedness with the divine which can speak to the human immediately only in symbol and myth. Tillich equated the death of the symbolic sense with the death of the sense of the sacred, worked in large part by theology's removal of the modern mind from the sense of its own divine ground or depth. His lifelong apologetic effort was based on the conviction that only the recovery of the sense of the sacred could make any particular religion, including Christianity, a truly meaningful and humanizing reality for the modern spirit.[10]

Thus, in their analysis of the impoverishment of contemporary spirituality through a theologically induced loss of a native sense of the sacred, Jung and Tillich share common ground. Moreover, both find a resonance in Heidegger's critique of modernity and its "forgetfulness of being." Heidegger, like Tillich, identified such "forgetfulness" in Aquinas and his tradition.[11] The superficiality induced by its removal from a sense of the holiness of being truncates humanity and reduces theology to ideological and

8. P. Tillich, *Dynamics of Faith* (New York: Harper, 1958), p. 45.

9. P. Tillich, "The Two Types of the Philosophy of Religion," *Theology of Culture,* ed. Robert C. Kimball (Oxford: Oxford Unviersity Press, 1959), p. 17.

10. *Ibid.*, p. 17.

11. Thomas F. O'Meara, O.P., "Heidegger and His Origins: Theological Perspectives," *Theological Studies,* 47, 1986, p. 218. O'Meara writes, "...Aquinas was a representative of the forgetfulness of Being, of the preference for beings."

self-interested pedantry divested of a redeeming depth. This seems to be Heidegger's thrust when he writes, "Even the famous *Summa Theologica* of Thomas Aquinas is a textbook - one for beginners..."[12]

Such an impoverished consciousness sterilizes not only the religious imagination but the reality of history by limiting the appearance of the sacred to sporadic divine intrusions then held as normative, as exhaustive of divine revelation, and usually as exclusive or preferential to the community thus questionably favoured. Religious impoverishment of this kind moves easily into religiously grounded social and political division with all its attendant dangers, culminating with our modern period in extensive loss of life when archetypally possessed communities encounter each other in geographic interface. All of these features combine, then, to uproot the individual from his or her natural experience of connectedness with the divine and to divest the collective human enterprise of an enlivening and unifying sense of its divine purposiveness. In one form or another, externalism, literalism and historicism still cling to the imagination operative in mainstream Christian reading of its own archetypal literature called biblical revelation.

Yet, in the interests of fairness and clarification, if one is to address Jung's critique of biblical imagination, one should first be able to give at least a brief sketch of the rudiments of the myth itself and of the manner in which the Christian imagination has come to respond to its story. Let us, then, attempt what is admittedly an unsophisticated, perhaps even naive, formulation of the commonly held major features in the biblically grounded Christian imagination of the nature of God and of the relation of that God to what is not wholly God, commonly called creation.

Though this summation may well appear simple, even artless, in relation to the immense scholarly and technical apparatus which has been invested in biblical research in the last century, nevertheless, what follows accurately reflects the impression that the common mind would carry away from exposure to the archetypal themes in the biblical narrative. It also reflects the orthodox theological elaboration of the narrative. In this sense

---

12.   M. Heidegger, *Schellings Abhandlung uber das Wesen der menschlichen Freiheit* (Tubingen: Fcick, 1971), p. 33f, cited from Thomas F. O'Meara, O.P., *op. cit.*, p. 220.

biblical fundamentalism has much to commend it in its precritical assumption that it alone remains faithful to the core of the revelation and embodies the simplicities of the myth which the gospels and their precedents in Jewish mythology represent. For the brunt of theological development of the original myth would appear to be little more than a sophisticated fundamentalism whose purpose, however concealed, remains always the simple affirmation that the myth is true and to be preferred to its competitors.

The Christian God at the centre of the myth is before all also a transcendent God. Transcendence, thus imagined, demands that the being of God is, at least potentially, discontinuous from the being of creation. This God could have remained in his eternal self-sufficiency. In the popular imagination which yet informs, however surreptitiously, even the best of Christian theological discourse on the nature of God's transcendence, this is the God who existed eternally before the world was created. Just how long before is never made explicit. "Before" is long enough to make the point at issue. As appropriated by traditional dogma and theology, this God creates from a state of supreme self-sufficiency *ex nihilo sui et subjecti*, "from nothing of himself or of a subject." This brief formula thus denies that creation contains in itself anything of the divine being or that divinity worked on any pre-existing or co-existing material in creating. Why such a God would bother and how the Christian theological imagination projects on his motives will be addressed below.

Such a God is perfect in all respects, and the Christian imagination reflecting on the biblical myth articulates this perfection in a variety of ways. There seem to be two major motifs in the Christian concern with God's perfection. The first is that it be unblemished with any taint of evil. This aspect of divine perfection, though of great importance, may remain secondary to another yet more important implication of divine perfection to the Christian mind. That implication is that the Christian God must act in creating without any sense of compulsion or necessity. All self-aggrandizement or the slightest hint of need by the creator in the act of creation is absolutely abhorrent to the imagination which has come to inform the myth.

This concern for divine purity and self-sufficiency, whatever its justification might be in the myth itself, became a significant contributor to the formulation of the presiding symbol within the myth, that of the Trinity. Over time, the myth, informed by these motifs, became the basis for the affirmation, through the elaboration of the Trinitarian dogma, that the opposition, which the dogma itself implies existed in the inner life of God, was eternally resolved in the perfect self-definition or expression of the Father in the Son or *Logos* and in the union of that expression with its source through the Holy Spirit. Thus in one way or another, Trinitarian doctrine is an affirmation that all tension between opposites within the divine life has been resolved in the unity of the Holy Spirit prior to creation and as its pre-condition. The successful resolution of the divine antinomy functions as the basis of an external self-sufficiency and serves as the precedent to its secondary expression in creation.

In certain theologies this resolution of the inner tension or contradiction within the divine life is understood as the motivation or dynamic for the expression of such eminently successful life externally in creation.[13] The dynamic operative in this paradigm suggests that Trinitarian life tends naturally to share the goodness of its balanced intensity, in accord with the theological maxim, *bonum sui diffusivum est*, "the good is diffusive of itself."

The Christian imagination, in a process that approaches self-deception, has historically been able to avoid two obvious difficulties in this paradigm. The first is that it comes perilously close to suggesting some "necessity" in God's sharing of his goodness with creation, even if such sharing be motivated by the best of intentions. This implied compulsion to share divine life beyond itself stands in some considerable tension with the

---

13.   *Cf.* St. Bonaventure, *Itinerarium Mentis ad Deum*, ch. 6, sec. 2, *The Mind's Road to God*, trans. George Boas (New York: Bobbs-Merrill, 1953), p. 39, where Bonaventure argues that the goodness of the unity of Trinitarian life naturally diffuses into creation. It is also present in Eckhart's doctrine of the *bullitio* and *ebullitio*, the boiling up within divine life which boils over into creation. *Cf.* Bernard McGinn, "Theological Summary," *Meister Eckhart* (New York: Paulist Press, 1981), pp. 39-45. The principle may be operative wherever the Christian imagination appropriated emmanational thinking, whose primordial or archetypal inspiration probably derives from Plato.

alleged self-sufficiency and inner contentment of Trinitarian life. The second difficulty is that this overflow of divine goodness in the form of a shared life whose intensity derives from the balanced harmonies of its reconciled opposites hardly finds a clear reflection in the human experience of existential life. Rather, in the lived experience of actual humanity, the contradictions in life seem hardly to be reflective of or responsive to the balanced unities of opposites and resultant vitality that the symbol of the Trinity stands for and should theoretically mediate.

Needless to say, reflection on the distance of existential humanity from the blessed balance of its trinitarian matrix brings up the problem of evil. As Jung clearly saw, this problem is in principle impossible of solution when creation and so human consciousness are viewed as an arbitrary by product of a divine life process complete in itself and allegedly sharing and reflecting its integrity in the creation of the unaccountably shattered other. Intimations such as these led Jung, as we shall see, to the possibility that the contradictions of existential life are the truest reflection of its ground and that, if they are to be overcome, their resolution is the task of history in interplay with its creative and conflicted precedent.

In another, though related, form of Christian imagination, trinitarian self-sufficiency and integration is experienced and depicted as the ultimate resource for the resolution of the potentially annihilating disruption or fragmentation which threatens created, existential life beyond its Trinitarian ground.[14] Such imagination is at the core of Paul Tillich's specifically trinitarian pantheism. In certain ways this paradigm is better equipped to take seriously humanity's experience of its suffering disintegration in existential life. However, to make it work, Tillich has to equate processes of humanity's, and of each human's, freely taken option to become conscious through a willful act of self-affirmation with original sin, now understood not as a past "historical" event but as a necessary and universal moment in the

---

14.   *Cf.* Paul Tillich, *Systematic Theology*, Vol. I (Chicago: University of Chicago Press, 1951), pp. 249-252, and Vol. III (Chicago: University of Chicago Press, 1963), pp. 283-294.

10

maturational process of the individual.[15]   When the same dialectic unfolds
from the perspective of God, Tillich has to argue that humanity, rooted in its
trinitarian matrix, was somehow absorbed in a "dreaming innocence" and so
was not quite real until it gained some fuller reality beyond its unqualified
essential unity with the Trinity, in and through the sin of willing to become
self-conscious.[16]   Tillich can then use this paradigm to establish an
experiential intimacy between God and humanity by contending that
humanity, in moving beyond its essential reality in God, never is severed
from its groundedness in God.   Its ambiguous experience of this
groundedness becomes for Tillich the basis of human eros as ultimate
concern for the recovery of that ground and so of one's essential humanity.
Again the paradigm is attractive in its ability to illuminate the ambiguities
and suffering of the human situation.   But again it contains elements that
clash with the myth and its traditional theological elaboration.   For it
demands that God necessarily create to break his dreaming innocence, that
he could not create an unfallen humanity since becoming fully human
involves an act of the will which severs each individual from an unqualified
unity with God and that humanity thus fallen never loses its sense of God,
and with Tillich, its native intimation of a specifically trinitarian God.[17]
Tillich's affirmation that atheism in the individual is as impossible as the
secular in society[18] implies a pantheism so radical that it imbues human
consciousness with traces of its connectedness with the flow of Trinitarian life
between its abyss and *logos* dimensions.

---

15.   Tillich works out these themes most explicitly in *Systematic Theology*, Vol. II
(Chicago: University of Chicago Press, 1957), part III, B, pp. 29-44.

16.   *Ibid.*, Vol. II, pp. 33-36.

17.   *Cf.* Paul Tillich, *Systematic Theology*, Vol. I (Chicago: Chicago University Press,
1951), p. 250. Tillich writes, "God's life is life as spirit, and the trinitarian principles are
moments within the process of the divine life. Human intuition of the divine always has
distinguished between the abyss of the divine (the element of power) and the fullness of its
content (the element of meaning), between the divine depth and *logos*."

18.   Paul Tillich, "The Two Types of Philosophy of Religion," *op. cit.*, p. 27. Tillich writes,
"...secular culture is essentially as impossible as atheism, because both presuppose the
unconditional element and both express ultimate concerns."

The dawn of consciousness understood as that point in which creation and fall coincide and so as "the original sin" has considerable resonance with foundational elements in Jung's paradigm of psychic development. Inasmuch as the ego breaks the unqualified and unconscious unity with its divine matrix, consciousness is created and with it the world. With Jung this creation is also a fall, for its birth from the unconscious imbues the ego and consciousness with the sense that it is removed, and painfully so, from the energies that both create and renew it. Therefore the ego is driven to recover its origins and renewing energies by re-entering the womb of the unconscious in a cyclical process which for Jung is the basic movement of psychic growth, a process without end in any given lifetime. Thus there is a substantial core agreement in Jung's psychology with Tillich's insight that the achievement of human consciousness is one in which "...creation and fall coincide."[19] Yet Tillich's insight, for all its brilliance and for its demonstrable sensitivity to the universal implication of consciousness in processes of suffering, alienation and disintegration, is hardly a position at the heart of theological orthodoxy. He seems himself to have acknowledged this when he would sign his portrait as "paganus Christianis," "a pagan to the Christians."

For these reasons it is understandable why it is only in the final pages of the third and last volume of his extensive *Systematic Theology* that Tillich explicitly introduces the idea of panentheism, obviously operative in the system from the outset, as the ontological and epistemological prerequisite of humanity's natural experience of God and of its trinitarian intimation.[20] No doubt Tillich's reticence in textually acknowledging anything like a pantheistic element in the ontology and epistemology which structures his system was due to his intuitive recognition that the timid Christian theological imagination could not tolerate a system founded on such experienced intimacy between the divine and the human. It is from this fear that Christian theologians continue to use the term "panentheism" rather than "pantheism" to describe the truth on which sensitive pantheism rests

19.   P. Tillich, *Systematic Theology*, Vol. II, *op. cit.,* p. 44.

20.   P. Tillich, *Systematic Theology*, Vol. III (Chicago: Chicago University Press, 1963), p. 421.

when not reduced by its Christian critics to absurdities it never held. That truth is grounded on the experience of those not cut off from it, not infrequently as victims of a superficial theology, of that point in each human where divinity and humanity naturally coincide.

Though Tillich may have only made it explicit late in the day, he must be credited with seeing the incompatibility, if not contradiction, between a wholly self-sufficient and transcendent God and any significant valuation of creation or of human consciousness. Tillich sought to close the breach by building a theology on the human experience of that point of inner being and life which humanity and deity share in common. But in his solution to the problem he violates the orthodox sense of divine transcendence in a number of ways. As shown above, it is obvious that a thinly disguised pantheism enlivens his theology with its sense of shared being and consciousness between the divine and human. He posits a need of God to create to become real, and of the human to will its separation from God to become real. While doing this, he clings to an experienced intimacy between the being of God and of the human mind. This intimacy is offensive to at least two of the major orthodox theologies. It would conflict with those theologies like Thomism which would prefer to eliminate such an experienced intimacy in favour of a supernaturalism or externalism which would divest the human of a sense of the sacred by denying that the continuity of being between the divine and the human breeds a universal sense of the divine. It would also be offensive to mainstream reformed traditions which argue that the corruption and sinfulness of humanity has divested it of any sense of the divinity which is operative in its redemption. Thus Tillich's theology is, at least in these crucial points, on its way to Jung's position, but remains in the end a halfway house not capable of fully accommodating the wholly other God of biblical imagination and orthodox theological reflection, nor the God of Jung's myth who is forced to create human consciousness in order to become self-conscious in it.

Returning to the Christian conception of divine perfection, considered now not from the viewpoint of self-sufficiency but from that of moral purity, it hardly needs repeating that the Christian God is one "in whom there is no darkness."[21] Though darkness and evil thoroughly pervade creation, they are not to be found in the creator. In classical Roman Catholic theology, for instance, the analogy of created being with the being of the creator may be extended to the shared traits of unity, truth and goodness, but cannot be extended to anything in creation that implies in itself imperfection, let alone evil. Yet, in accord with the orthodox telling, the humanity which proceeded from the hand of such a good, omnipotent and omniscient source, as itself perfect, turned against its creator and implicated itself in a fall whose consequences were universal. Somehow the Christian imagination was able to avoid the obvious implication that the analogy of being should be extended to the analogy of evil and locate created evil and created good in the one source of all being, as does Jung. Rather, it was able to convince itself that the fall in no way compromised the goodness of the creator. It was due solely to the corruption of the product and not the producer.

When literalized, this fall is depicted as that unfortunate event in which an originally perfect couple turned against their perfect creator. Teilhard de Chardin, not without a sense of humour, comments on the initial rejection of a perfect God by a perfect couple, when he writes "...one can only regard the Creator as having been extremely unlucky."[22] Teilhard, fully aware of the irony in this remark, spent much of his life in developing a coherent world view in which God, understood as a unifying force, entered into the reversal of disintegrating powers out of the frank need, in Teilhard's mind, for self-completion in the Pleroma in and through the evolutionary process.[23] Humanity's potentially universal experience of the reality of this divine energy now working in and through the human psyche toward the further unification of humanity becomes for Teilhard the basis of an

---

21.   I John 1:5. Cited by Jung in "Answer to Job," CW 11, par. 698, p. 435.

22.   Teilhard de Chardin, "Reflections on Original Sin," *Christianity and Evolution*, trans. R. Hague (London: Collins, 1971), p. 193.

23.   These positions taken by Teilhard early in his career remained unchanged throughout his lifetime. *Cf*. his early summations in "La lutte contre la multitude" (1917) and "L'Union creatrice" (1917) in *Ecrits du temps de la guerre* (Paris: Bernard Grasset, 1965), pp. 109-132 and pp. 169-198.

14

energizing pantheism which grounds his cosmology. Thus he pushed Christianity to "baptize"[24] pantheism in the interest of the recovery of that vision he describes when he writes, "*nothing* here below is *profane* for those who know how to see."[25] When these views surfaced and were understood in the early twenties, Teilhard was exiled to China and eventually died unpublished, a tragic witness to the power of biblical and theological-dogmatic literalism working through Roman Catholic power structures.[26] Given the sense of mutual inhesion that Teilhard sought to recover in the divine-human relation, it is interesting to note that Teilhard's works were known to be in Jung's possession and on his reading list at the time of Jung's death.

Thus, it is clear that the brunt of Christian imagination across denominational lines imbues the events of creation and fall with a strange and inexplicable arbitrariness on the part of both creator and creature. The myth goes on to extend this arbitrariness to the creator's response to what Teilhard describes as his initial bad luck. Just as the creator arbitrarily creates a perfect original couple who somehow implicate the totality in turning against him, he equally arbitrarily sends a saviour, his Son, the *Logos*, in a unique historical incident which not infrequently in the Christian imagination and myth is held as the definitive, and so final or exhaustive, revelation. Like the Father himself, this Son is without spot or blemish and contests successfully with a demonic power who is as absolutely evil as the Son is good. In his triumph all share or can share as all have fallen in the original fall.

This Son, though the object of widespread rejection and the sufferer of a cruel death, will return, again at an arbitrary time but now in power, in

---

24.   *Cf.* "Mon Univers," (1918) *Ecrits du temps de la guerre, op. cit.*, p. 278. Teilhard writes, "La tendance au pantheisme est trop universelle et trop tenace pour qu'il n'y ait pas, en elle, une ame de verite (naturellement chretienne) qu'il fait 'baptiser'."

25.   Teilhard de Chardin, *Le Milieu Divin* (London: Collins, 1960), p. 66.

26.   For an excellent account of the silencing of Teilhard and his removal from France, *cf.* Mary and Ellen Lukas, *Teilhard: The Man, The Priest, The Scientist* (New York: Doubleday, 1977), part I, The Burning Bush, ch. 6, pp. 69-75, and pp. 85-96.

what Jung describes as the transformation of the lamb into the ram,[27] and separate humanity into the saved and rejected. A split humanity will be eternalized but without significant effect on the divine well-being of the self-sufficient Trinitarian Godhead who presides over the entire drama and who is no more enhanced by its ambivalent initiation than he will be diminished by its eternally divided finale.

All of these statements represent the main lines of orthodox Christian belief. They would find widespread acceptance across denominational borders at a level deeper than institutional arrangements surrounding such concerns as the means of grace and intramural discipline. Jung, in the deepest level of his spirit and of his mature thought, could appreciate all of them and accept none of them. In fact, his whole psychology must be understood as a reversal and an appreciative undermining of the myth whose rudiments these previous formulations try to capture.

Turning then to Jung's psychology, what precisely are the elements which undermine even as they appreciate the central motifs in the Christian myth? The foundational undermining element, if it were to be put into theological language, is the way Jung relates the immanent to the transcendent in his psychology. For Jung the reality of God is a function of the psyche and is based on the experience of the numinous.[28] Such experience is thoroughly immanent insomuch as it is generated by archetypal powers in that dimension of the psyche Jung terms the collective unconscious. This dimension of the psyche precedes and gives birth to the ego and its consciousness and at the same time seeks to become itself fully conscious in its creature. Jung understands the experience of the numinous to be a consequence of the impact of these archetypal energies on the ego quite independently of its will. Jung writes of such experience, "...it seizes and controls the human subject, who is always rather its victim than its

---

27.   "Answer to Job," CW 11, par. 708, p. 437. Jung writes, "We no longer recognize the meek Lamb who lets himself be led unresistingly to the slaughter; there is only the aggressive and irascible ram whose rage can at last be vented."

28.   C. G. Jung, "Psychology and Religion," CW 11, par. 6, p. 7; par. 9, p. 8.

16

creator."[29] While humanity is universally susceptible to the experience of faith understood as the impact of the numinous on consciousness, the origin of this faith is never the ego, and so remains in some legitimate sense for Jung a transcendent event and reality in the sense that such faith owes its origins to powers within the psyche which transcend the ego.

Thus, only in the experience by the ego of those powers which transcend it in the unconscious stratum of the psyche can one establish a legitimate sense of the transcendent in Jung's psychology. His psychology does not tolerate the intrusion into the psyche of realities or forces which originate beyond it, though he does admittedly extend the boundaries of the unconscious to the infinite. The epistemology which attaches to Jung's metaphysic, always operative in spite of his repeated denials that his psychology contains no metaphysic whatever, assumes the psyche to be an organic unity and that all consciousness, that is the knowable, derives from its inner working. This is the import of such allegedly non-metaphysical statements which Jung so frequently makes as "Not only does the psyche exist, it is existence itself."[30]

Any such extra-psychic force as a wholly transcendent God inorganically related to the psyche would, at best, remain unknowable in principle to the psyche or, at worst, do violence to the psyche's organic integrity through its intrusion into it from beyond. But it is precisely in such intrusions that the biblical imagination understands the reality of various divine calls to individuals and societies as the bases of intra-historical redemptive programs. These divine incursions can extend to the designation of certain peoples as chosen, on occasion, not without the benefit of divinely endowed land grants.

For the Christian this intrusive process culminates in the Incarnation, which in turn will culminate in a final judgment, itself, at least in the imagery of its apocalyptic formulations, bearing no organic relation to processes of history. As an aside, one might wonder if the violence implied in such divine

29. *Ibid.*, par. 6, p. 7.

30. *Ibid.*, par. 18, p. 12.

intrusion on the human from beyond the human is not related to the violence which quickly surrounded the Christian myth in its historical development almost as soon as the means of violence were available. This violence continues to manifest currently in the connection of death with monotheistic transcendentalism wherever conflicting one and only Gods face each other through their chosen in geographical proximity. The furthest reach of this line of speculation might well point to a dawning moral sense that would identify monotheistic faiths in transcendental Gods as themselves of questionable moral social value whose removal or attenuation may become a condition for collective survival.

Unlike the individual's relation to the wholly transcendent God depicted in the Christian imagination as potentially ontologically discontinuous from creation, in Jung's paradigm the ego can never be ontologically severed from its unconscious precedent. Thus it cannot be wholly removed from the possible and, effectively, inevitable experience of the faith-creating archetypal persuasion of the unconscious which can so easily take on the form of individual or collective possession.

Rather than impoverish humanity's religious sense or become the basis of a form of psychological reductionism, this relation of consciousness to its creative source would mean that, for Jung, efforts to get the sense of God out of the psyche are in fact impossible. Where attempted, such efforts could succeed only at the cost of depriving the victim of a living contact with those divine but profoundly ambiguous energies which both fund life with the sense of its own goodness and can equally well destroy it through the truncation of a one-sided possession. Unfortunately, such a collectively diminished state of consciousness is still, too often, understood by theologian or political demagogue as the substance of faith and the committed life. In either case the result would be an uprooted psychic life susceptible on the one hand to the agony of the superficial, and, on the other, to various forms of unperceived archetypal possession which move into the faith void and generate a faith consciousness which becomes the enemy and not the servant of the humanity it possesses, individual or social.

This native connectedness of human consciousness with the source of the sense of the sacred opens Jung's psychology to the truth of the

18

ontological argument in its historical formulations both before and after Anselm's classic twelfth century statement.[31] Put succinctly, the argument would be that the only "proof" for God's existence is humanity's ineradicable and unmediated experience of God. This experience Jung locates in the interplay between the forces of the unconscious and a responding consciousness. On these grounds Jung equates the practice of religion with the "scrupulous observation" or "careful consideration" of that which addresses consciousness from the unconscious.[32] In doing so, he implies that such observation can and should come to function as a dialogue between the ego and those powers which, throughout human history, have given birth to the Gods and Goddesses and which continue to address the individual through the dream on a nightly basis.

For Jung, then, creation occurs when the ego is born from its unconscious matrix and revelation occurs when the ego turns first to listen and then to respond to the continued overtures of its unconscious precedent and generator. Thus, from the perspective of Jung's psychology, just as ego and the unconscious can never escape their natural relatedness since they share the same being, neither can humanity and divinity. This would be as impossible as affirming that the unconscious could exist without creating consciousness as the vehicle and locus of its own becoming conscious.

On this point Jung would stand with Meister Eckhart's spirit in the latter's affirmation that creation is from eternity, that is, that it derives from God as a natural and inevitable consequence of the being and activity of God. In fact, in an early discussion of Eckhart's theology, Jung uses Eckhart as the occasion to develop his own theory of relativity to best describe the relation between the divine and the human.[33] In unpacking what he means by his theory of relativity, Jung states explicitly what we have above suggested

---

31. C. G. Jung, *Psychological Types*, CW 6, pars. 59-63, pp. 39-43. *Cf*. Paul Tillich's almost identical treatment of the ontological argument in *Systematic Theology*, Vol. I, *op. cit.*, pp. 204-208.

32. C. G. Jung, "Psychology and Religion," CW 11, pars. 6, 8, pp. 7, 8.

33. C. G. Jung, "The Relativity of the God-concept in Meister Eckhart," *Psychological Types*, CW 6, pars. 407-431, pp. 241-256.

about the natural connectedness of the ego with the unconscious which is for Jung the basis of humanity's connectedness with divinity. Jung writes, "...it [the theory of relativity] also implies a reciprocal and essential relation between man and God, whereby man can be understood as a function of God, and God as a psychological function of man."[34] As functions of each other it is obvious that for Jung humanity and divinity are naturally linked in being and this link is the basis of the epistemic inevitability of the human sense of God.

The metaphysical intimacy which Jung thus establishes between the divine and the human denies the knowability of a God who is wholly other and the possibility of a benign relation of such a God to the human psyche. But Jung's counter myth does more, for it moves beyond the corrosion of this foundational element in the Christian imagination to an undermining of Christianity's central symbol, that of the Trinity. In doing this Jung's psychology dissolves the imagination which attaches to the symbol of the Trinity as an eternally self-sufficient God in whom there is no shadow. This aspect of Jung's myth, though far from unrelated to the intimacy which he establishes between divinity and humanity, is of even greater importance in the conversation between his psychology and the Christian imagination.

Though Trinitarian speculation may be somewhat remote or oblique even for Christian minds, it seems to have held a certain fascination for Jung from early childhood years. He informs us in his autobiography of his anticipation of his minister father's treatment of the topic in preparation for his confirmation. He goes on to relate his disappointment in his father's brushing aside of the dogma with the remark that he, his father, did not understand it himself.[35] Looking back on the incident from old age, Jung saw in it an early intimation of the pathologizing severance of experience from belief in the world of official dogma and theology.

---

34. *Ibid.*, par. 412, p. 243.

35. C. G. Jung, *Memories, Dreams, Reflections* (New York: Vintage Books, 1961), pp. 52, 53.

20

In his mature years Jung went on to write one of his major essays on the symbol of the Trinity.[36] It is in this essay that one sees most explicitly the radical paradigm shift at the heart of Jung's psychology. This shift constitutes a powerful alternative to the Christian imagination grounded on its central symbol of a Trinitarian God. At the heart of the new paradigm is Jung's move from a Trinitarian to a quaternitarian view of psychic and so of all reality. In the early section of this key essay Jung reflects on the meaning of triadic patterns as they recur in a number of religious mythologies, and in major philosophers such as Pythagoras and Plato.[37] In doing this Jung is being faithful to his archetypal methodology which would demand that any archetypal expression such as that of the Trinity can be better understood to the extent that its historical variants are surfaced in the interests of mutual elucidation.

The major conclusion Jung draws from this survey is that the triad is a symbol which expresses the ground movement of the psyche itself. Thus the reality of the Father, the furthest reach of the Trinity, becomes the world of the unconscious vested with an infinite power and fecundity but divested of discriminatory consciousness. The reality of the Son or *logos* becomes the world of consciousness born of the unconscious or Father world but in residual tension with it. The Holy Spirit becomes the connecting and reconciling link, the realized unity and harmony of the potentially warring opposites, namely the unconscious as generator and its child or effluent, consciousness.[38] In this context the realization of the Spirit as both the cause and product of the unity of consciousness with the unconscious can legitimately be called the goal of psychic development.

In passing, it is worth noting a subtle but crucial point Jung makes in the conclusion of this essay, which further elucidates his understanding of the self-contained nature of the process of individuation as symbolized by the

---

36. C. G. Jung, "A Psychological Approach to the Dogma of the Trinity," CW 11, pp. 109-200.

37. *Ibid.*, pp. 112-128.

38. *Ibid.*, pp. 129-137.

Trinity and excludes from it any intervention of an extra-psychic power. He makes this point through the expression of his deep appreciation of that ecclesial reflection which came to understand the inter-relation of the three persons of the Trinity in terms of its concept of *homoousia* as of the same nature, as equally divine. Had the ecclesial formulation not done so, it would be for Jung a statement of disequilibrium which would mute or neglect some integral aspect of the organic unity of the fundamental psychic dynamism which births consciousness from the unconscious and works throughout to make them one.[39] Here again is blatant evidence that Jung understands the theological expression, *homoousia*, as an expression of psychological truth whose meaning is that the unconscious, consciousness and their movement toward unity in the Spirit are of the same nature, or are one organic process.

As Jung elaborates the substance of this psychological truth in his formulation of the quaternity, it becomes a clear statement that the processes of maturation which the symbol of the Trinity expresses point to an understanding of human maturation that is wholly intra-psychic individually and intra-historical collectively. Put simply, the symbol points to the self-contained nature and dynamic of the psyche itself insomuch as its unconscious ground differentiates and then seeks to reunite its opposites in human consciousness historically and individually. Through his reflection on the *homoousia*, Jung makes it clear that this process does not require, indeed would be violated by, a point of reference somehow transcendent to it.

To this point in the essay, Jung's position is simply that the psychological significance of the symbol of the Trinity lies in its reflecting to consciousness the most basic movement of the psyche itself, namely of the reciprocity between the unconscious and the ego. Yet it should be noticed that even here Jung has taken the symbol of the Trinity out of its wholly transcendent framework by making human consciousness, in effect, the second moment in the Trinitarian procession and the locus in which the first principle of the Trinity becomes conscious.

Then Jung introduces a final section to the essay with the question of the fourth, and in so doing he wholly removes his psychology from a

---

39.　　*Ibid.*, par. 289, pp. 194, 195.

22

Trinitarian pattern at least as understood in a manner compatible with Christian orthodoxy.[40] Here his basic argument is that the ultimate source of creativity within the Trinity, in traditional language, the Father, is only credited by the symbol of Trinity with a one-sided creation both within and beyond Trinitarian life. For while the spiritual, the good and the masculine are there, the material which in this context would encompass the bodily and the instinctual, as well as the demonic or evil and the feminine, is not.

Jung's response to this real absence is to indict a Trinitarian paradigm which intends to depict the fullness of either divine or created reality with a self-discrediting one-sidedness. His response is to reconceive divine life and its created expression in a quaternitarian pattern. In this pattern the first creative principle, the one, is as alive with creative potential as it is divested of the power of rational discrimination. This is the state Jung, in a playful gnostic poem, calls the Pleroma.[41] In it the opposites which conflict with and yet belong to each other in conscious life are in a state Jung calls "contamination." This means the opposites are not differentiated because there is no point of consciousness in such a condition. As consciousness is propelled from this cauldron, it becomes the second principle in the divine drama, but might equally well be described as the second and third. This is so because its discriminatory power severs the opposites which remain only partly distinguished in the unconscious. In so doing, consciousness makes the conflictual potential in the unconscious conscious. Deity for the first time can become aware of its self-contradiction.

It is out of this imaginal framework that Jung describes the suffering of human historical consciousness. For such consciousness comes to realize that the unconscious ground which has given it birth is itself unreconciled in its opposites and seeks the resolution of its self-contradiction in human

40.   *Ibid.*, pp. 164-192.

41.   "Septem Sermones ad Mortuos" in Memories, Dreams, Reflections, op. cit., pp. 380, 381, for instance. It is interesting to note here that, though the term "Pleroma" is central to the thought of Teilhard and Jung, it functions with opposite meanings in each system. For Teilhard it points to an eschatological consciousness and love and so is an endpoint. For Jung it is a synonym for the creative power of the unconscious seeking consciousness for its realization and so is a point of departure easily associated with the Goddess as creative.

consciousness. In Jung's opinion this is the stage of religious development reached and depicted in the biblical *Book of Job*. In it human consciousness is brought to the horrifying awareness that its deepest meaning and moral responsibility is to unite in itself consciously the powerful and contradictory opposites in the divine nature which God could neither perceive nor unite in himself. Jung writes, "Job realizes God's inner antinomy, and in the light of this realization his knowledge attains a divine numinosity."[42]

At the heart of Job's numinous experience was the realization that Yaweh was a living antinomy, whose turbulent life consisted in suffering the vagaries, swings of emotion and arbitrariness which attached to such living self-contradiction. For Jung, Job's realization accounts for Job's conscious and moral superiority to his creator even if he remained in a much less enviable position in terms of power. Thus for Jung, the divine failure to bring order into its life is the ultimate reason for the creation of humanity and its discriminatory consciousness. Indeed, such divine irresponsibility, unmasked in Job's religious experience, becomes not only the ground reason for creation but also the motive for the Incarnation, understood now as God's desire to become as conscious and responsible as Job through immersion in Job's suffering the experience of being the creature of such a conflicted God. All of this is implied in Jung's reconception of the commerce between divinity and humanity and of the motive of Incarnation when he writes "...the father wants to become the son, God wants to become man, the amoral wants to become exclusively good, the unconscious wants to become consciously responsible."[43]

To spell out the metaphysical and theological import of the foundational elements of Jung's psychology pertinent to this discussion, it must be said that God is not fully conscious and so not self-sufficient within the flow of Trinitarian life from eternity. God is rather embroiled in a contradiction defiant of solution on an intra-Trinitarian basis. God thus creates out of a certain necessity, impelled by the need first to become

---

42.   C. G. Jung, "Answer to Job," CW 11, par. 584, p. 377.

43.   *Ibid.*, par. 675, p. 424.

conscious, through human consciousness, of his inner contradiction and its irresolution on the level of what has been traditionally imaged as the inner life of God, and then to seek the resolution of the divine contradiction in that same human consciousness.

For Jung the age of the Son, the present state of our consciousness, is an age of conflict not only with the Father but also with the contradictory absolutes that, though they be grounded in the Father and have a relative legitimacy, split individual lives and have from the outset bloodied history. The age of the Spirit symbolizes that eschatological state of consciousness, for Jung the culmination of the deepest native drive of the psyche, in which the opposites born from the undifferentiated One into their conflictual realization in human consciousness achieve their final unity there. For Jung this is the meaning of the eschaton, but it is also an *apocastastasis*, in Origen's sense, for it demands a recapitulation in a final harmony of all the potentialities which exist in the unconscious.[44] Anything less would imply that God had failed to give full expression to his potential in his culminating realization in human consciousness.

There are certain major opposites in the life of the psyche and so of God which Jung identifies as clamouring most loudly for their unification in the age of the Spirit. Thus the tension between the masculine and feminine might look to the symbol of the androgyne which has long served as a pointer to the resolution of this conflict in eschatological consciousness. The age of the Spirit would also have to work a consciousness in which the physical and the spiritual were experienced as one. In his work with Wolfgang Pauli, the noted Nobel prize-winning physicist, Jung was led to wonder if the so-called material and the spiritual did not belong to each other in the unconscious, which could and did work to compensate excesses in either direction in consciousness. In the famous extended imagery in which Jung relates these opposites to the colours in the spectrum, he associates red with pure instinctuality, blue, by implication, with pure spirituality, and ultra-violet, the

---

44.   C. G. Jung, *Letters* (Princeton: Princeton University Press, 1973, 2 vols.), vol. 1, p. 541. Letter to Victor White, December 31, 1949. Here Jung refers to Origen and aligns himself with Origen's thought that, "...the devil might be redeemed."

unity of blue and red, with the synthesis between instinct and spirit which the unconscious would seem to promote and demand.[45] In this way the unity of matter and spirit as grounded in the unconscious and seeking unity in conscious life is not beyond the imagination.

The final unity which Jung's psychology envisages in the age of the Spirit is that between the figures of Christ and Satan. Under the still presiding power of biblical imagination, even to imagine either their embrace or common origin continues to be impossible. Yet it would be in the resolution of this seemingly irreconcilable opposition that Jung's psychology presents Christianity with one of its greatest challenges. By extension this challenge has a much wider reach than simply uniting split absolutes within one mythology. In the contemporary climate the problem is constellated most dramatically in the absolute splits in political life and between international power blocks. In this manner has the split between Christ and Satan moved beyond the Christian myth to wider and more powerful constituencies.

Before addressing this problem and what Jung's understanding of the psyche might have to offer in its resolution, some further remarks should be made about the theological implications of the economy operative in the dialogue between the ego and the unconscious as Jung conceives it. These theological implications touch on such traditional topics as the nature of redemption and the priority of God in the gracing of humanity. From what has been exposed to this point, it is obvious that, in Jung's myth and metaphysic, God and humanity are not only naturally and necessarily linked in their being and consciousness of each other but that they are involved in a process which can only be called one of mutual redemption. The intricate dialectic that Jung establishes between the ego and the unconscious engages the ego in a dialogue with the unconscious whose purpose is the ushering into consciousness of the unconscious in the incarnation of the self. That Jung uses such a religiously laden term as "incarnation" to describe the process

---

45.   C. G. Jung, "On the Nature of Psychic Energy," CW 8, pars. 414-418, pp. 211-215.

signals the religious import he attributes to it.[46] The conscious realization of the self is the *telos*, the goal, of the all-encompassing psychological process Jung calls individuation. At its heart is the unity of the ego with the unconscious in the emergence of that "supraordinate"[47] or "more compendious personality"[48] in whom the self is progressively born.

Jung understands this to be a process painful to both the unconscious and to the ego. From the viewpoint of the unconscious Jung likens entrance into finitude to the famous passage in Philippians 2:6-11 that attributes such great humility to the Christ figure for abandoning his divine prerogative and taking on creaturehood in the form of a slave.[49] In his work on Job, Jung makes the same point even more dramatically when he writes, "That is to say, God wants to become man, but not quite."[50] On the other hand, the tortures of the cross and worse are for Jung symbolic depictions of the suffering which the ego must undergo, not once, but repeatedly throughout the course of a lifetime, if it is constantly to die toward an ever fuller incorporation of the self. Avoidance of this suffering through a theology of vicarious atonement, which would magically locate in the life of a past historical figure and event the agony that each individual must undergo at the hands of the self in the interests of its incarnation, remains for Jung an evasion of the pain of life and the growth it demands and a further consequence of Christian externalism and historicism.[51]

---

46.   *Cf.* C. G. Jung, "Transformation Symbolism in the Mass," CW 11, "The Sacrificer," pp. 261-265, for the best description of this process in terms of the "incarnation" of the unconscious in consciousness.

47.   C. G. Jung, "A Psychological Approach to the Dogma of the Trinity," CW 11, par. 276, p. 185.

48.   C. G. Jung, "Transformation Symbolism in the Mass," CW 11, par. 390, p. 258.

49.   *Cf. ibid.*, p. 293, fn. 59.

50.   C. G. Jung, "Answer to Job," CW 11, par. 740, p. 456.

51.   C. G. Jung, "Transformation Symbolism in the Mass," CW 11, pars. 409-413, pp. 271-273.

Faithful to this reciprocity at the heart of Jung's psychology, one must say that the ego, in cooperating with the unconscious in its incarnation, both creates and redeems the divine. This dialectic is again elaborated in Jung's understanding of the true meaning of the alchemical enterprise. For Jung the *aureus non vulgus*, "the non vulgar gold" sought by the alchemist, is the emergence into consciousness of the self, understood as the unity of consciousness and the unconscious. In his alchemical writings he makes it explicit that the self is the *filius philosophorum*, the "son" or creation of the "philosopher," that is, the son or creation of the individual who enters into conscious dialogue with the unconscious with the purpose of ushering it into consciousness. To put this point into clear religious language, Jung is here stating unequivocally that the individual in dialogue with God enables God to become conscious and thus real in the consciousness of the individual in whom the self is realized and to the extent that it is realized. Yet it is equally true that the ego of the alchemist is itself the son or creation of the unconscious, which from this viewpoint is the father or mother or generator of all consciousness.[52] Put succinctly, the dialectic at the heart of Jung's psychology is one in which the unconscious creates consciousness in order to become conscious, that is, created and redeemed in it, in a process which unites and completes both.

This is again explicit in Jung's alchemical works when he describes the unconscious as the *deus absconditus*, the hidden or dark God, who is redeemed into consciousness from his own immersion in matter, used here as a synonym for unconsciousness, through the co-operative efforts of the alchemist.[53] Thus understood, the process of individuation is in and of itself a sacred endeavour. Through it God becomes conscious of his totality, of its contradictions and of their reconciliation in human consciousness. God's redemption from divine unconsciousness necessarily involves a process in which the full extent of the opposites in the ground of being and consciousness are made painfully conscious as they work toward their

52. *Ibid.*, par. 400, p. 263, where this dialectic is succinctly exposed.

53. C. G. Jung, "The Visions of Zosimus," CW 13, pars. 138-139, pp. 104-105.

conscious embrace in humanity. Thus does Jung's soteriology, his understanding of redemption, confer upon the human co-operator with the divine an importance and initiative that few Christian theological reflections on the nature of redemption can. Nor was Jung unaware of the heresy in his thought. Aniela Jaffe's remarks have much to commend them when she writes, "From the viewpoint of dogmatic Christianity, Jung was distinctly an 'outsider'...More than once he said grimly, 'they would have burned me as a heretic in the Middle Ages.'"[54]

Yet Jung's psychology does retain a certain sense in which the ego remains, throughout the process of individuation, subordinate to a superior power in a manner reminiscent of the insistence of Paul, Augustine and Luther on the priority of God in every moment of the gracing of the human. This transcendence attaches to the self, which presides over the entire drama even as it seeks realization in it. If the process Jung seeks to describe at the heart of the dynamic of psychic maturation is taken sequentially, first the self propels the ego from its matrix in the unconscious and then seeks ever greater entrance into the ego by working the marriage between the ego and the unconscious. This leads to the legitimate question of the self's intent toward the ego and of the effects of its becoming consciously incorporated in the ego. For Jung this intent is summed up in wholeness, and it is the self's drive toward conscious wholeness which empowers the process of compensation, as Jung understands it, to work at both the individual level in the form of the dream and at the collective level in the form of revelation.

Thus, in parallel processes whose dynamics are identical, the self works toward conscious wholeness in the individual through the preferred medium of the dream and in the collective through established religions, or, one might better say, through religions that became established because the revelations they bore were recognized by the unconscious of the collective they addressed as the needed compensating answer to whatever aspect of the human plight was dominant in that society. One might say with equal justification from this side of Jung's thought that just as the individual is sent the dream he or she needs and deserves, so also is society sent the saviour it

---

[54].   Aniela Jaffe, "Introduction," *Memories, Dreams, Reflections, op. cit.,* pp. x, xi.

needs and deserves. The revelation which gives to its religion also provides that culture with its needed compensation toward wholeness.

We have already dealt with Jung's conception of relativity in his understanding of humanity and divinity as ontological functions of each other. In a somewhat similar sense his reflection on religions as collective compensations for their receiving societies also relativizes them and their founders. Jung brings this relativization to bear on Christianity and on the Christ figure.

Consistent with the understanding of revelation as collective compensation, he interprets the birth of the Christian myth as meeting the demand of the collective unconscious for a spiritual religion with the power needed to offset the enormous libidinal forces then mounting an assault on human dignity and life. In this context he appreciates Christianity and its sister religion Mithraism as much needed and restraining expressions of human spirituality whose successful containment of libido contributed to the building of our Western culture.[55] But then he asks if the restraining spirituality of Christianity does not now itself require a compensation in the recovery of the very forces and energies then needing repression. In effect this would mean a resacralization and reintegration of those major factors excluded from the Trinity, namely the material, the feminine and the demonic.

A different, though related, reflection on the compensatory genesis of the Christian myth and the need for its current supercession locates the myth in the context of the evolution of religious consciousness. Especially in his work on Job, Jung contends that Christianity's specific contribution to the development of religious consciousness is its perception of the absolute opposition between good and evil, personified in its myth by the undying opposition between Christ and Satan. He writes of their absolute opposition but common heritage in these terms: "Just as Satan plays the role of accuser and slanderer, so Christ, God's other son, plays the role of advocate and

---

55.   C. G. Jung, *Symbols of Transformation*, CW 5, pars. 103-104, pp. 59-70.

30

defender."[56] For this reason, Jung occasionally mourns the possible loss of the Christian myth before it was understood, i.e., before the absolute contradiction in the ground of being to which it points through the opposition of Christ and Satan was made abundantly clear to its constituency.[57]

Yet in Jung's mind this awareness of the ongoing war between forces of absolute good and evil within and beyond the Godhead, though Christianity's greatest contribution to the evolution of religious consciousness, is precisely the reason that it cannot be the final myth. For the externalization of the split it establishes would mean a defeat for the spirit of the self, which works always to differentiate in order to unite. Final differentiation into opposing communities of the saved and the damned would thus defeat the power of the self to unify what it differentiates and so would also be a defeat and impoverishment for a creating God who by implication could not recover fully in the end what he had launched in the beginning, another way of saying that such a God could never become fully conscious.

Jung was also keenly aware of the social evils involved in myths pitting absolute evil against absolute good. If one lives in the atmosphere of a myth based upon such a split, it is almost impossible to avoid identifying with absolute good and projecting absolute evil onto one's contradictor or opponent. Indeed, this divisiveness, the identification of the hated other as ultimate threat, often seems to be the purpose of the myth in bonding communities of common belief.

Reflection on this side of Jung's psychology leads easily to the truly painful question, "Can communities be bonded without archetypal bonding, and, if not, how can they escape archetypally inspired hatred and fear for those who do not share in their cohering myth?" Jung clearly perceived the dubious social consequences of mythical consciousness which split the believing community from the demonized other. He was well aware that the

56. C. G. Jung, *"Answer to Job,"* CW 11, par. 684, p. 428.

57. C. G. Jung, *Letters, op. cit.,* vol. 2, p. 137. Letter to Victor White, November 24, 1953, where Jung speaks of the "lack of responsibility" in depriving "our fellow beings" of "a vitally necessary symbol" before its meaning was assimilated.

limited acceptance such faith inspired continued to prevail in an age when myth had lost its specifically religious hold over people only to re-emerge in political guise with little diminution of its potential for identifying its holders with absolute good and its negators with the devil. Whether a solution to this problem is contained in his psychology raises immense questions. Its basis is there in the universal empathy he experienced in the master symbols of the self, all of which imply the individual's experienced unity with the totality. Whether time remains for the dissemination of such a universalistic consciousness, even if it be the basic thrust of the deeper psyche as Jung contends, becomes the question of human survival in the face of the divisive limited faiths which currently petrify the development of humanity's collective psyche and threaten its continuation.

In the context of the twentieth-century psychic epidemics which broke out on the basis of the archetypally empowered "isms" associated with the names of Stalin and Hitler, Jung writes and underlines, *"The future of mankind very much depends upon the recognition of the shadow."*[58] The truth of Jung's insight here is born out by the fact that even in the latter part of the twentieth century one can hear talk of an "evil Empire" in places of immense political power. Had an author writing on the fundamentals of Jung's conception of the projection of the collective or political shadow placed these words in the mouth of a modern leader, such an author, until recently, might well have been accused of overreaching in the concoction of a draconian example to make a dubious psychological point and then summarily dismissed. It is now apparent that we no longer have the right to such dismay.

What directions then, does Jung proffer, in moving beyond myths such as Christianity, claiming to be final or exhaustive, but grounded on the dramatic split of absolute opposites within themselves, which fund the projections that engender communities of murderous division in history? What more encompassing empathy and what means for its attainment does Jung hold out beyond such divisive faith, whose circumscribed charity has driven our collective humanity to question the very basis of its hope?

---

58. C. G. Jung, *Letters*, vol. 1, *op. cit.*, p. 541. Letter to Victor White, December 31, 1949.

Fully to address this question requires the introduction of aspects of Jung's psychology which are hostile to at least two pillars of current cultural consciousness. The first is the penchant of collective consciousness for collective solutions to all human problems. The second is the current need for a conscious clarity about the outcome of a course of action prior to its being undertaken and the assurance that the solution to any and every problem lies wholly within the powers of consciousness, i.e. human knowledge and will.

Regarding the first point, exclusively collective approaches to humanity's problems, a foundational element in Jung's thought is that only the individual is the bearer of consciousness and particularly of the consciousness of the new. Such an approach would argue that the most effective way to prevent a recurrence of the Nuremberg rally would be through the dissuasion of each individual Nazi. Jung's implication is that once communal faith has metastasized in the possessed or believing community as little can be done for an individual in it as for a cell in a cancerous organ.

Such an approach also implies that only the individual can fully enter that realm from which the power of a newer mythical consciousness arises. Thus, if a consciousness is to evolve capable of healing the splits in the Christian myth and, by extension, the splits caused by the projection of absolute good and absolute evil by any individual or community on another, Jung would locate the process in the individual's dialogue with his or her own unconscious. From that direction is the individual to derive the resolution of conflictual opposites with that resultant wholeness which the self endorses and demands for that individual. In this manner does the individual move toward a consciousness which offsets both the pathology of personal one-sidedness and the pathological one-sidedness inherited through birth into a one-sided mythology, or religion, or their modern continuators, in the form of political, social or economic ideology.

In this manner would Jung conceive of the discovery of one's own truth and myth as the most significant contribution the individual could make to the transcending of personal pathology or a pathologizing collective myth, which not infrequently combine in a joint attack on the individual. Indeed, he would argue further that the making conscious of one's own myth is the deepest thrust of God's intent in history. Success in the discovery or recovery of one's deepest truth in this sense holds out the greatest promise of personal meaning and value because it is a process of the redemption of God through the grappling with that side of the divine self-contradiction which appears to the fore in the specifics of one's personal life and history. Wherever this struggle is engaged on a prolonged basis, the resultant transformation cannot but affect external life and so is rarely without social consequence, even though such consequence may remain a by-product of personal transformation.

Even supposing that such sustained dialogue be undertaken, what delineation can be given to the new myth and the consciousness that might emerge as healing the cleavages in our current myth? This question and its demand address the clarity of goal and assurance of the adequacy of the powers of reason and will in the working of all solutions which modernity seems to need as a precedent to action. For Jung the challenge of giving clearly stated substance to what a more widespread realization of the self would look like societally is not one he can too easily meet. The implications of his psychology seem to defy wooden political implementation, though they bear an immense political import. Jung might well respond to such inquiry that it is a little like asking what resurrection is like prior to being crucified when the manifest intent of the question is a transparent attempt to avoid crucifixion through intellectually constructing what may lie beyond it.

Perhaps the essential features of his reply are contained in the correspondence he carried on with Victor White, the English Dominican priest, throughout their relationship from 1945 until White's death in 1960. Here he gives what definitive shape can be given to his understanding of what might be involved in the appreciative transcendence and so undermining of our current religiously based dividedness.[59] He takes the position that such a surpassing consciousness, one that might unite, for example, the symbols of Christ and Satan, can only legitimately emerge from

59.   *Ibid.*, vol. 2, especially the letters of November 24, 1953 (pp. 133-138) and April 10, 1954 (pp. 163-174).

an honest, personal suffering of the archetypal contradiction between absolute good and absolute evil so dramatically depicted at the core of the Christian story. This explains Jung's fondness for the image of the Christ figure dying a tortured death between the opposites of a yes and a no, an affirmation and negation grounded in the ambivalent nature of the creator and creation.[60] It also explains Jung's shocking statement that only in his crucifixion did the Christ figure achieve any self-consciousness and that this self-consciousness was the substance of God's answer to Job.[61] Thus the substance of God's answer to Job, according to Jung, is that wherever any human suffers to the death the divine contradiction as it appears in his or her life, in that suffering itself humanity and divinity are redeemed to a resurrected consciousness. In this manner are divine and human suffering identified without residue when legitimately born toward a consciousness which resolved in itself the apparently irreconcilable opposites which sunder unredeemed and, so to speak, pre-resurrected life. Jung writes, "The whole world is God's suffering, and every individual man who wants to get anywhere near his own wholeness knows that this is the way of the cross."[62]

In other revealing passages in his correspondence with White, Jung addresses the problem more concretely. He commends as strongly as possible the living of the Christian myth and its one-sided values until their very one-sidedness forces the death of the effort.[63] In continuity with this theme, the death of an all too good, indeed unreal, figure striving for a conscious moral perfection is a significant side of Jung's interpretation of the death of Christ. In one of his gnostic writings Jung comments perhaps not

---

60. C. G. Jung, "Answer to Job," CW 11, par. 659, p. 417; par. 739, p. 455; and "Christ a Symbol of the Self," *Aion*, CW 9ii, par. 79, p. 44.

61. C. G. Jung, "Answer to Job," CW 11, par. 647, p. 408.

62. C. G. Jung, "A Psychological Approach to the Dogma of the Trinity," CW 11, par. 265, p. 179.

63. *Cf.* the letter of November 24, 1953, *op. cit.,* p. 136, and 138, where he insists that the symbol of Christ is valid until invalidated by the Holy Spirit, and the letter of April 10, 1954 (p. 167), where he likens crucifixion to death to the opposites and into a new age where God and man are one.

without a note of sardonic wisdom "...Christ is the perfect man who is crucified. One could hardly think of a truer picture of the goal of ethical endeavor."[64] But in all of this there is no hint of a conscious or deliberate abandonment of Christian consciousness or moral effort. In fact, just the opposite is the case. Such consciousness and effort, argues Jung, once constellated as an individual's religious fate, can only be legitimately surpassed through living out their impossible demands to the point where a more inclusive consciousness appears beyond the death of the old. Symbolically, the going beyond or resurrecting into a more unified consciousness is only by way of the cross, the suffering through to the psychic death of the contradiction of the old to the newness of a broader resurrected empathy.

This means that for Jung the harmonies of a resurrected consciousness can neither be conceived nor achieved by the powers of consciousness, that is by the ego and its powers of reason and will. The price of such harmony is adequately symbolized in the Christian mystery by death, in whatever form that death might take, in the service of the ushering in of individual and collective transformation characterized by a more embracing empathy. All this is implied in Jung's brief but oft repeated statement, *tertium non datur*,[65] "the third is not given." By it he means that the third, as the resolution of the suffering caused by archetypally grounded opposites, is never given to consciousness and its powers through their own operation. Consciousness can find it only on the far side of death, induced by its hanging between whatever form of the divine contradiction engages it, and not as the consequence of its reasoning or will.

Yet the conscious cultivation of a widespread, voluntary and individual undertaking of this death to a divided and dividing consciousness may now be a personal and collective necessity in the strategy for survival. The alternative would consist in that all too prevalent but dangerous lassitude in which the opposites continue to be literalized in competing

64.   C. G. Jung, "Christ, a Symbol of the Self," *Aion*, CW 9ii, par. 124, p. 69.

65.   *Cf.* for instance, C. G. Jung, "Answer to Job," par. 738, p. 454.

communities based on faith and proclaiming love but filled with hate for those differently possessed. Should such constellations continue to concretize, they could terminate the human adventure before its ground became fully conscious in it, in a final fury of divine and human failure.

In contrast to this option, an examination of the implications of what Jung took to be the master images of the self reveals what his mind and spirit came to understand as the culminating consciousness toward which the human psyche moves and which its nature demands. In a reversal of mainstream theological conceptions of divine transcendence, Jung saw in the symbol of the mandala an unmistakable acknowledgment of the sacred centre of each life, that point where the divine and the human naturally coincide. This implies for Jung that the centre of each individual's psyche coincides with the creative centre of the universe. He was fond of repeating the idiom that appears in Bonaventure and elsewhere in medieval tradition to the effect that "God is a circle whose centre is everywhere and circumference nowhere."[66] This imagery would clearly indicate that as each life moves closer to its centre, it relates out of that proximity to the totality of reality which is also a created expression of that centre. He writes of the individual who experiences this dimension of humanity, "He is of the same essence as the universe, and his own mid-point is its centre."[67] He goes on to describe such unity of the individual with a centre coincident with that of the universe as "...the goal of man's salvation and exaltation..."[68] Returning to the earlier discussion of externalism and the inorganic relation of divinity to humanity which such externalism carries with it, mandalic consciousness demands the negation of such discontinuities toward a sense of divinity as the natural core of each individual's humanity and to an understanding of the meaning of life as a progressive drawing nearer to that core.

---

66. C. G. Jung, "A Psychological Approach to the Dogma of the Trinity," CW 11, p. 155, fn. 6.

67. C. G. Jung, "Transformation Symbolism in the Mass," CW 11, par. 440, p. 288.

68. Ibid., par. 445, p. 292.

In his understanding of the *anthropos* image, Jung describes a consciousness in which each individual feels his or her unity with the totality of all that is human and with the human totality. Here he simply shifts emphasis to a microcosmic-macrocosmic model and implies that unity with one's centre unites the individual with humanity itself. Likewise, in his conception of synchronicity with the help of alchemical imagery, which would find significant resonances in the history of Western philosophical thought, he visualized a "ground of all empirical being."[69] This ground could orchestrate patterns of meaning in the lives of individuals defiant of the laws of probability. Such synchronistic events Jung understood to be in the service of a more endemic, less sporadic synchronous consciousness. Such synchronistic events would set a life thus touched on the road to the realization of its meaningful connectedness with all that is through contact with the source of the all in the depth of one's personal being. Jung is obviously here referring to a consciousness aware of its living out of God and seeing oneself and all that is as transparent to the sacred. Yet he shows it to be a most human and natural state, the natural culmination of human maturation.

Thus the consciousness that attaches to the sense of the self unites elements that are often viewed as opposites. These seeming opposite effects, the unification of the individual's internal multiplicity, the complexes, within the boundaries of one's personality and an extended relatedness to reality beyond the boundaries of individuality, are for Jung the dual hallmarks of the entrance of the self into any life. For the self brings about a unity of the many potentially conflicting powers that make up our empirical personalities, and as it does, it relates the individual thus blessed through a much extended empathy to an ever more encompassing totality. One is progressively enabled to say a more enthusiastic yes to more.

The reason for these dual but ever present aspects of the consciousness borne by the self might find its best philosophical expression in

---

69. C. G. Jung, *Mysterium Coniunctionis*, CW 14, par. 760, p. 534.

38

nineteenth-century German idealism and romanticism.[70] The experience
would have to be expressed in a formulation which could capture the idea
that the matrix out of which the world is born is immediately accessible in the
depths of each personal life and seeks to become conscious in that life. As it
does so, it makes that life whole by unifying it on its own basis and relating it
to the totality beyond itself, because such a life is in the process of being
pervaded by the origin of all individuality and so of the totality. In this
respect current work on Jung's relation to this tradition might make a
significant contribution to the philosophical elucidation of the implications of
the self and its whole-making and empathy-extending potentialities.

Yet the process is a suffering one, because the source of life is also the
generator of life's most destructive oppositions. The Christian myth makes
this obvious. The question now is whether humanity will suffer these
contradictions internally, spiritually and psychically, as the legitimate way of
moving beyond them to the experience of those unities which Jung
understands the psyche to intend and toward whose conscious appropriation
it is driven by its own deepest dynamic. This, as Jung puts it in one of his
letters to White, would be a process in which the symbol of Christ might be
currently invalidated by the same Holy Spirit which constellated it.[71] In the
same letter he sums up his whole thought on the process of Christianity's
surpassing itself when he writes, "The state of the Holy Spirit means a
restitution of the original oneness of the unconscious on the level of
consciousness."[72] Here Christ and Satan would have to embrace, since both
are valid components of "the original oneness."

In this understanding of the psyche's deepest movement to the "state
of the Holy Spirit," Jung would push Christianity and all myths, which divide
community from community, or which uproot consciousness internally and

---

70. Work in this area is currently in progress. *Cf.* for instance, S. Kelly's work,
Individuation and the Absolute: Hegel, Jung, and the Path Toward Complex Holism. Ph.D
thesis, Department of Religious Studies, Ottawa University, defended, May 1988.

71. C. G. Jung, *Letters, op. cit.*, vol. 2, p. 138, November 24, 1953.

72. *Ibid.*, p. 135.

spiritually from a living sense of its universal and natural divinity, to see what resources they might have within themselves to transcend themselves. At this point Jung's critique of Christianity and other mono-myths becomes the question he asks of them all: "What resources do you have to lose your divisive faiths in time to save our collective humanity?"

Should this question be pursued and asked insistently, it could reveal that the quiet power of the self may yet prove to be our greatest resource. For by its nature the self moves us to a broader empathy informed by a much livelier sense of our common origin in the divine. It also brings to us the sense of the incessant pressure of the divine as that primordial energy empowering our common human task of redeeming it in history. As the self thus understood incarnates more broadly in our common humanity, it will provide it with a more universal sympathy than our current traditions, religious or political, can easily mediate. Hopefully such broadened and deepened sensitivity, gained through immediate dialogue with its divine sponsor in the depths of our common humanity, will become for all traditions a conscious goal before whose sacred allure we and they can jointly bow.

Before such gracious wisdom can be first experienced and then consciously surfaced, humanity would have to grow familiar with its presence in its depth. For Jung this meant the recovery of the sense of the Goddess in and through whose dissolving and resolving energies the newer myth might surface. This aspect of Jung's spirit makes of him one of the early twentieth-century recoverers of the Goddess in her most radical presence and power. The consequences of this recovery and the hope it provides humanity can now be addressed.

CHAPTER TWO

THE GODDESS AS MOTHER OF THE TRINITY

Jung's break with Freud was dramatically aided by a dream which he interpreted to point to a dimension of the unconscious deeper and more encompassing than Freud's psychology could accommodate.[1] The dream was devoid of overt religious implications, yet it was of immense help to Jung in more ways than simply precipitating his break with Freud. It was an early and significant step in moving Jung toward his more mature formulations of psychic maturation. In these later formulations Jung came to describe psychological maturity as the individual's experience of greater individual integration coupled with the sense of nearing identity with the totality. Needless to say, such experience carried with it an empathy moving to the embrace of the whole.

Especially in the more precise formulations of his later works did Jung come to explicit statements that the experience of wholeness he sought to describe, by its own dynamic and nature, combined the experience of personal unification with universal relatedness. These apparently opposite experiences, personal integrity and universal relatedness, were made possible and necessary in the process of maturation because its base dynamic was towards the individual's experience of unity with "...the eternal Ground of all

---

1.   The dream is described in C. G. Jung, *Memories, Dreams, Reflections* (New York: Random House, 1961), pp. 158, 159.

empirical being..."[2] as the ground of one's individual being and consciousness. As Jung came to his mature delineations of this experience, he clearly affirmed that unity with this ground served to centre the individual on his or her external reality in the ground of all and to relate the individual to the all through that ground. As such, it was at once the most intense form of religious experience and the culmination of psychic growth. In these specifically Jungian categories human maturation and religious maturity become one without differentiation.

The dream which, in Jung's estimate, contributed so significantly to these later directions, placed Jung in a room at ground level in a house which had a series of lower rooms. The deeper Jung descended into these subterranean layers, the further he penetrated the past, period by period, age by age. At the depth of his descent he came upon two skulls lying in a cave at the foot of descending stone stairs. In this primordial setting Jung felt the dream had led him through the various stages of human development to the origins of humanity itself. Moreover, and most importantly, it had shown him the living connection of his current consciousness to these stages and to their primordial origin within his own psyche. Though his ego, the centre of his personal consciousness, lived in the twentieth century in Switzerland, its roots extended through the total experience of humanity to the dawn of consciousness and, perhaps, beyond to its animal precedents.

The individual's sense of continuity with even the animal past is more than implied in one of Jung's reflections on his experience in Africa. Standing on a low hill overlooking a savanna teeming to the horizon with animal life, he felt that his and humanity's self-consciousness was the product of what he saw before him and that what he saw before him was, in some sense, "created" by humanity's self-conscious sense of organic continuity with it. In effect, Jung is affirming, in these passages, that the evolutionary process becomes self-conscious in human consciousness. Reflecting on the experience, he writes, "Human consciousness created objective existence and

2. C. G. Jung, *Mysterium Coniunctionis*, CW 11, par. 760, p. 534.

meaning and man found his indispensable place in the great process of being."[3]

For Jung humanity's "indispensable place" by no means implied that human reflective consciousness had severed its continuity with its natural precedent. Rather, he suggests that all levels of historical life, even the pre-human, become fully aware of themselves in human consciousness, whose culminating maturational experience is then one of conscious continuity with the totality of being and life at every evolutionary level of their realization. In a manner reminiscent of nineteenth-century German romanticism and idealism and of some streams of modern evolutionary theory,[4] the paradigm Jung here proposes would strongly suggest that the creative ground of each centre of now living human consciousness has initiated the process leading to human consciousness to become aware of itself in human consciousness.

As he amplified the meaning of the dream over the years, Jung was to conclude that this dream, re-enforced by other psychological indicators, pointed to the presence in each individual of a living bond to the source of all consciousness, historical and personal. He was to write of the impact of this dream, "It was my first inkling of a collective a priori beneath the personal psyche."[5] This "inkling" was to grow into Jung's later conviction that the "a priori" source of all consciousness beneath our personal centres of consciousness was imbued with an overriding passion driving it to seek entrance into fuller consciousness in each individual's life and in the process of history itself. Thus, the ingression of the source of all consciousness into historical consciousness became for Jung the meaning and destiny of each individual life, and by extension, the meaning of history itself.

---

3. C. G. Jung, *Memories, Dreams, Reflections, op. cit.,* p. 256.

4. This creator-human paradigm has profound affinity with the vision of Teilhard de Chardin, whose works Jung was reading at the time of his death.

5. *Ibid.,* p. 161.

Jung explored this deeper dimension of the psyche initially in Volume 5 of the current *Collected Works*.[6] This work extended the psyche in ways that defied its reduction to consciousness or reason as either possible or to be desired. In thus extending the parameters of the psyche to dimensions that consciousness could not exhaust, Jung guaranteed his break with Freud. It meant that reason could neither ultimately control, absorb, nor reduce to itself that which had given rise to it, just as it could never free itself from the possibility and inevitability of numinous address by its intra-psychic matrix. Insistence on the existence and functional priority of this dimension of the psyche became the foundational differentiation of Jung's psychology from Freud's and from the latter's assertion that in the end consciousness, reason and science could reign fully independently and in control of that which preceded and gave birth to consciousness.[7] Jung's experience of this dimension of the psyche drove him to the use of language pointing to the psyche as itself a process in which a potential infinity sought its realization in human consciousness in a manner which denied to the latter a dictatorial control within its own psychic house.[8]

Jung's grounding of individual consciousness in the potentially inexhaustible is textually explicit and serves as one of the most important distinguishing features of the spirit of Jung's psychology when read organically. This spirit is, for instance, most evident when Jung describes the unconscious as "...of indefinite extent with no assignable limits..."[9] or again in the same passage when he states bluntly that the unconscious is "...by

---

6.   C. G. Jung, *Symbols of Transformation*, CW 5 (Princeton: Princeton University Press, 1956).

7.   The supremacy of reason is particularly evident in Freud's late works, *The Future of an Illusion*, trans. W. D. Robson-Scott, ed. J. Strachey (London: Hogarth Press, 1978) and *Civilization and Its Discontents*, trans. Joan Riviere, ed. J. Strachey (London: Hogarth Press, 1969).

8.   The dialectic of an "unlimited" unconscious with the ego is well described in "Transformation Symbolism in the Mass," par. 390, pp. 256-259, especially on p. 258.

9.   *Ibid.*, CW 11, par. 390, p. 258.

definition unlimited...."[10]   Jung's thrust in these passages is that the unconscious, precisely because of its inexhaustible fecundity, can never be encompassed or fully realized in any individual psyche.   For Jung the ego remains always in dialogue with a power greater than itself whose conscious actualization in any given life can only be approximated, never exhausted by the ego in the process of the individual's maturation.   When the dialectic of individuation is examined in this light, Jung would seem to be describing a process of maturation which can never be more than one of approximation. This understanding of maturation carries with it the stark implication that the demand to realize the self cannot be evaded without self-betrayal, even as it would reduce the contention that the self had been fully realized in any life to one of self-deception.   The suffering involved in living out this paradox constitutes the glory, the pain and the ultimate dignity of becoming fully human.

Though it might appear inappropriate to more literal minds, it is worth reflecting on the gender of this unlimited and creative largesse which, for Jung, is the deepest ground of the psyche and seeks to become fully realized in consciousness, its child.   Jung's more mundane term for this deepest dimension of the psyche was the "collective unconscious." Yet in pointing to its reality and power, Jung has opened up to the twentieth century the possibility of the recovery of a sense of the Goddess which, when fully appropriated, can make less radical understandings of her nature and power look trivial and, when she is depicted as one among many deities rather than their common source, self-defeating.

As his thought on this dimension of the psyche matured through his more extensive experience of it, Jung came to describe the collective unconscious as the "matrix mind" from which all historical consciousness is born.[11] In doing this Jung moved to imagery which combines the notions of the maternal and the intensely creative as best capturing his understanding of

---

10.   *Ibid.*

11.   Jung's classical references to the matrix and matrix mind are: "On 'The Tibetan Book of the Great Liberation,'" CW 11, pars. 781, 782, p. 490 and par. 790, p. 495; "Foreword to Suzuki's 'Introduction to Zen Buddhism,'" CW 11, par. 899, p. 552.

this deepest dimension of the psyche. For from this matrix mind arise not only consciousness itself but also its most meaningful and enduring statements in the form of the myths, religions, philosophies, political configurations, the great works of literature, and, indeed, all the significant expressions of the human spirit which both grace and can destroy consciousness but whose surfacing it cannot evade.

In his alchemical work Jung was to call this dimension of the psyche, as did some alchemical traditions, the *prima materia*,[12] the matter from which all consciousness arises. This *materia* is destined, when transformed through its incarnation in consciousness, to become the prized *aurum non vulgus*,[13] the golden consciousness of the self born of the marriage of the ego with its unconscious precedent and creative matrix. The consciousness thus born moves, in the life of the individual and of humanity collectively, by the native rhythm of the psyche itself toward a sympathy as extensive as the embrace of the matrix mind which creates it and, in turn, seeks to become fully conscious in it. Thus Jung's conception of the unconscious as the mother both of consciousness itself and of its enduring statements contains a profound dialectic in which the mother of consciousness creates consciousness in order to become real in it. The teleology which derives from this dialectic and informs Jung's psychology and mythology throughout describes the drive of each individual's psyche toward an empathic unity with the totality born of the individual's conscious appropriation of the source of that totality from the depths of one's personal being. In this manner does the mother of all consciousness seek to become real in each individual centre of consciousness in a process of mutual completion.

These ground themes in Jung's psychology suggest that what Jung, through the many formulations of his life's work, is striving to delineate as the reality of the collective unconscious simply is the "Great Mother," the

---

12.   *Cf.* C. G. Jung, *Mysterium Coniunctionis*, CW 14, par. 246, p. 193, where Jung relates the *prima materia* to the sea and to the "matrix," by implication as mother. *Cf.* also *ibid.*, par. 15, p. 21f, where he explicitly describes the *prima materia* in its feminine aspect as the "...moon, the mother of all things...."

13.   *Cf.* for example, *Psychology and Alchemy*, CW 12, par. 40, p. 34.

"Goddess" herself. For in her most majestic and numinous form it is she who creates, destroys and renews human consciousness, and who shapes the ground movement of human history, personal and collective, in her efforts to become ever more fully incarnate in it. This makes of Jung one of the earliest and still more significant twentieth-century recoverers of the Goddess, not in one or other of her concrete and so lesser manifestations, but in her primordial nature as the source of consciousness itself and of all that can become significantly conscious. Since Jung unequivocally equates psyche with being,[14] this would mean that for him the Goddess is the source of all that is and can be because she is the source of both consciousness and of all of its substantial expressions.

In his sustained efforts to reroot humanity in her demanding but ultimately sustaining powers, Jung thus becomes one of the earliest and more insightful critics of the modern cultural blight called patriarchal consciousness.[15] As the term is used by Jung in the context of the specifics of his psychology, it refers to every form of consciousness which prefers to remain within itself, to rely exclusively on its rational powers and willful energies and, so, to refuse the invitation of the Goddess to death and renewal in a life-long process with which the ego can and must co-operate but never control.

Jung thus functionally equates the ego's entry into the unconscious with access to the Goddess and so makes of it a religious event, in whatever manner it might occur. It is not surprising then that Jung's elaboration of the specific meaning of patriarchy and patriarchalism in the context of his psychology occurs in his religious writings. An analysis of the texts in which the terms appear in his *Collected Works* and letters reveals both the

---

14.   *Cf.* "Psychology and Religion," CW 11, par. 18, p. 12, where Jung writes, "Not only does the psyche exist, it is existence itself."

15.   For Jung's textual critique of patriarchalism *cf.*, "A Psychological Approach to the Doctrine of the Trinity," CW 11, par. 223, p. 151; "Answer to Job," CW 11, par. 627, p. 399; *ibid.*, par. 753, p. 465, where Jung describes Protestant Christianity and Mithraism as "...a *man's religion*..."; letter to Adolf Keller, March 20, 1951, C. G. Jung Letters, Volume 2, 1951-1961, eds. Gerhard Adler, Aniela Jaffe, trans. R. F. C. Hull (Princeton: Princeton University Press, 1974), p. 9, where he associates Protestantism with "...the patriarchal line of the Old Testament."

48

consistency and radical nature of his understanding of patriarchy and so of the radical transformation of individual and societal consciousness that would be currently demanded as an alternative to it.

In his work on the Trinity[16] Jung argues in his opening position that the Trinity can be appreciated as a symbol of the ground movement of the psyche itself. Thus the symbol points to that process which is foundational to all of Jung's psychology, the process he terms "individuation." Viewed from the perspective of Trinitarian symbolism, the major movements of individuation become the differentiation of consciousness (the Son or Logos) from its creative preceding in the unconscious (the Father) and the conscious reunion of these opposites in the emergence of the self (the Holy Spirit).[17] Even at the level of this preliminary reflection, Jung pays the symbol of the Trinity the highest of compliments in suggesting that it reflects to consciousness the basic movement of the psyche itself. In doing this, the symbol reveals to consciousness its role in the psyche's movement toward becoming whole. This movement always seeks, and is ideally realized in, the harmonious flow of energy between the ego and its unconscious precedent involved in the emergence of the self as that state of consciousness in which the unconscious becomes more progressively incarnate in consciousness. It is interesting to note that in his essay on the Mass Jung can describe this same process in terms of the death of the ego into the unconscious through its suffering of archetypal conflict and its resurrection or return to consciousness with an empathy of wider embrace.[18] By the fact that he describes the unity of the ego with the unconscious in the making of the self as "incarnation," Jung reveals that he considers it always a religious event and indeed close to the substance of religion itself.[19]

16. *Cf.* "A Psychological Approach to the Doctrine of the Trinity," CW 12, p. 109f.

17. *Ibid.*, sec. 2, pp. 129-137 and sec. 4, pp. 148-163.

18. C. G. Jung, "Transformation Symbolism in the Mass," CW 11, especially sec. 4, p. 247f.

19. *Ibid.*, *Cf.* Jung's section on parallels to the Mass p. 222f, and par. 338, p. 221.

Yet, in the latter and crucial part of the essay on the Trinity, Jung moves to a criticism of the symbol of the Trinity and what it implies for the movement of the psyche. Here he argues that it be superceded by the symbol of the quaternity.[20] In doing this, Jung posits as the deepest dimension of the psyche a creative source, itself without definition, yet the source of all that can take definition in consciousness and especially all that can take definition in the form of the conflictual opposites which both enliven and threaten conscious life. In this transition Jung reacquaints Western imagination, however surreptitiously, with the reality of the Goddess as that creative matrix out of whom all opposites come seeking first their differentiation and then their resolution in human consciousness.

The move to the quaternity and its reintroduction of the Goddess as the mother of consciousness and the opposites consciousness bears implies three crucial points in how Jung reconceives and re-experiences the divine human relationship in this paradigm shift.

1.   The divine creatrix of consciousness is not self-sufficient in her own life. The source of consciousness must create it to perceive and then resolve in consciousness her own unresolved ambivalence.

2.   The relationship between consciousness and its divine matrix is one of organic continuity. Consciousness is of its nature in ontological continuity with its creator Goddess. In this move Jung, in effect, introduces a fourth element into the dynamic of deity, namely, human consciousness itself. To make the implications of this point explicit to traditional Christian consciousness and imagination, one might point to the older traditional paradigm in which the Son necessarily proceeds from the Father and is united with the Father in Spirit in an external resolution of opposites preceding creation. This is not the case in Jung's quaternitarian paradigm. In it human consciousness proceeds necessarily from its divine conflictual source as the place where the conflict is first recognized and then resolved in the Spirit, now understood as the resolution in human consciousness of the divine contradiction which gives consciousness necessary birth.

---

20.   "A Psychological Approach to the Doctrine of the Trinity," sec. 5, pp. 164-192.

3.   Since the Goddess is the source of all opposition and creates in order to resolve these oppositions in consciousness, any significant form of consciousness, especially religious, which is not capable of deifying both opposites in any polarity, including that of male and female, is one-sided and so pathologizing.

In his shift to a quaternitarian model of the psyche, Jung has in effect denied the core implication of Trinitarian symbolism, that is, that the opposites in the divine life, the Father-Son split in Christian imagery, have been eternally overcome as the pre-condition to creation. To the contrary, Jung argues that such a conception of a perfect God wholly other or transcendent to the human is a key motif in patriarchal religion and morality, especially social morality. Jung writes, "There can be no doubt that the doctrine of the Trinity originally corresponded with a patriarchal order of society."[21] In amplifying this remark Jung refers to both the Christian and Islamic traditions and implies, when his argument is fully analyzed, that they are both patriarchal because they rest on the idea of wholly transcendent, monotheistic and perfect Gods, inevitably male, whose demands on the human are harsh because of the divine expectation that the creature become as perfect, and so as one-sided, as the masculine deity himself. Jung's "Answer to Job"[22] focuses on the contradiction implied in the traditional depiction of the divine-human relationship in which a perfect creator both omnipotent and omniscient is so consistently disturbed by the bad behaviour of his flawed creatures. In this work Jung moves to locate the basis of the flaw in the creator as preceding and reflected in his flawed creation.

Jung's reflections on trinity and quaternity at least raise the question as to why the three wholly transcendent "one and only" monotheistic Gods, Yaweh, Allah and the Christian Trinity, are so consistently masculine. It would seem that the more removed from their genesis in the Goddess the deities become through processes which function to make them wholly transcendental and monotheistic, the more masculinized they turn out to be.

---

21.   *Ibid.*, par. 223, p. 151.

22.   "Answer to Job," CW 11, p. 365f.

When this process is subjected to a fully psychological analysis, it is revealed to be one which produces male and wholly transcendental Gods each with a claim to monotheistic, universal exclusivism because, at heart, it is a process of uprooting consciousness from its experiential connectedness with the unconscious and so with the more inclusive creativity and empathy of the Goddess. Put briefly, no centre of consciousness in living touch with the God-creating agency, the unconscious, could long remain convinced that God could be only masculine.

Largely on the basis of the association his psychology establishes between masculinity and a heightened sense of divine transcendence attached to the wholly other God, Jung identifies such demanding and yet sterile perfection in the divine as a hallmark of patriarchal consciousness. He writes about this development, "no path leads beyond perfection into the future - there is only a turning back, a collapse of the ideal, which could easily have been avoided by paying attention to the feminine idea of completeness."[23] Again, within the context of his psychology, Jung can show why patriarchal values are so sterile by describing or defining the essential note of patriarchal consciousness as the severance of the conscious mind, male or female, from the experience of its native rootedness in the unconscious, its creator and renewer. In short, the emergence of wholly other, transcendent and perfect Gods in the development of human religiosity is linked to psychological processes which sever their victims from the Goddess and so from the life that religion claims to foster.

Were these male Gods to be reintegrated with the powers in the psyche to which they owe their existence, they could not retain their exclusive masculinity, because the psyche is not only the source of our sense of divinity but also of all the opposites that appear in known reality, including the male and female. Thus, retracing divinity to its origins in the psyche is at once to recover the sense of the feminine as divine and to go beyond even this recovery to the experience of the deepest level from which consciousness is born as infinitely creative and thus maternal. The recovery of this cosmic maternity as the ground of both individual and collective consciousness is the

---

23. *Ibid.*, par. 627, p. 399.

52

deepest meaning of the recovery of the reality and power of the Goddess. In this sense Jung could not have uncovered the reality of the collective unconscious without reappropriating for modernity the primacy of the Goddess.

It is not surprising, then, that Jung's indictment of patriarchy becomes an indictment of the exclusion of the feminine in its full range of expression in mainstream Christianity and other forms of uprooting monotheisms. When read organically, his psychology links the Christian God "in whom there is no darkness"[24] to Christ as equally perfect and so unreal[25] and to the figure of Mary deprived of her full humanity through the doctrine of her sinlessness and virgin birth. "Both mother and son are not real human beings at all, but gods."[26]

This side of Jung's critique of Christianity and of Catholic Marian doctrine indicts its God, its messiah and its leading feminine figure with a spiritual one-sidedness and so pathologizing incompletion. Summing up this side of his critique, Jung writes, "Yaweh's perfectionism is carried over from the Old Testament into the New, and despite all the recognition and glorification of the feminine principle this never prevailed against patriarchal supremacy."[27] To these remarks he adds a note anticipating in 1952 the critique of religious patriarchy which the following decades were to produce, "We have not, therefore, by any means heard the last of it."[28]

In the interests of presenting Jung's total response to the depiction of the feminine in the Christian myth, one has to introduce a second theme that parallels his critique of the one-sided purity of the Christian God, of the

24.   *Ibid.*, par. 698, p. 435.

25.   A typical passage addressing the one-sidedness of the ethically perfect Christ is to be found in "Christ, a Symbol of the Self," CW 9ii, p. 69. Jung writes, "The Christ-image fully corresponds to this situation: Christ is the perfect man who is crucified. One could hardly think of a truer picture of the goal of ethical endeavor."

26.   "Answer to Job," CW 11, par. 626, p. 339.

27.   *Ibid.*, par. 627, p. 399.

28.   *Ibid.*

messiah and of his virgin-mother. This theme is that the figure of Mary *is* a figure of a Goddess. Patriarchal theological reasoning may bend over backward to distinguish the status of Christ as alone divine and Mary as the first among saints. In Jung's view the unconscious laughs at such distinctions. Jung is well aware that "according to the dogmatic view" Mary is not a "goddess." Nevertheless, when her status is given archetypal value, she is for Jung "...functionally on a par with Christ, the king and mediator."[29]

It cannot then be denied that Jung saw in the declaration of the Assumption which he considered to be "...the most important religious event since the Reformation"[30] an effective recovery, at least within Roman Christianity, of the religious reality of the Goddess, incomplete though she remained through her one-sided purity. Moreover, in the context of Jungian psychology this event functions as a new revelation. For Jung's psychology contains within itself a psycho-theology of revelation as such. In his understanding of the psyche, revelation occurs when the unconscious provides that powerful compensation necessary to correct the dehumanizing imbalances in collective consciousness and culture. Thus, revelation is for Jung a product of the compensatory function of the collective unconscious redressing the pathologizing one-sidedness of the collectivity which both demands and receives such revelation. When these points are considered, then, Jung's delight with the doctrine of the Assumption is grounded on his conviction that it represented a powerful, though admittedly incomplete, compensation to patriarchal cultural and religious consciousness. The consequences of the Catholic declaration for Jung served to indict Protestant and, indeed, any dissent to the truth of the newly proclaimed Goddess as patriarchal, literal, rationalistic, and ultimately incapable of comprehending either religious experience or its symbolic expression. All of this is contained in a typical passage.

> The logical consistency of the papal declaration cannot be surpassed, and it leaves Protestantism with the odium of being nothing but a *man's religion* which allows no metaphysical

---

29.   *Ibid.*, par. 754, p. 465.

30.   *Ibid.*, par. 752, p. 464.

> representation of woman...Protestantism has obviously not
> given sufficient attention to the signs of the time which
> obviously point to the equality of women.[31]

As suggested, the term "Protestantism" is used here by Jung in a sense that
could include certain streams of empirical and institutional Protestantism but
whose meaning is extended to all religious forms of thought imprisoned in an
exclusively conscious, rational, historical approach to religious reality and its
development.

Since, then, mutual penetration between our conscious personality
and the Goddess, its creator, is the substance, the very core, of the process of
individuation and so of Jung's psychology when read organically, it is of some
import to examine the specifics of such self-renewing incest. If one is to
speak of the creation of consciousness in sequential or temporal terms as the
Jewish and Christian imaginations have taught us, one must image the
Goddess in her most powerful and primordial state as "prior" to the advent of
consciousness. As this primordial reality, the Goddess exists as that
Pleroma,[32] the primal uroboros, in which all that can be defined and split in
consciousness seethes and boils in that state of indifferentiation Jung terms
contamination.[33] It is in this sense that the Goddess or great Mother needs
to give birth to her child, consciousness, as that power in which her opposites
are first differentiated and then, with her help and that of the self, reunited in
ever wealthier and more embracing states of consciousness.

Yet even, or perhaps especially, at this level of his myth does Jung
first strike the note of the Goddess' ambivalence. For in her primal
plenitude are found all the forces which later split into good and evil, light
and dark, spiritual and material, male and female, indeed into all the
opposites that divide and can destroy individual and community in finite
existence. In her, too, are to be found all those archetypal powers, with their

31.   *Ibid.*, par. 753, p. 465.

32.   *Cf.* "Septem Sermones ad Mortuos," *Memories, Dreams, Reflections, op. cit.*, p. 379f,
where Jung links the "pleroma" with a primordial "nothingness."

33.   C. G. Jung, "On 'The Tibetan Book of The Dead,'" CW 11, par. 738, p. 491 and par.
817, p. 504.

inescapable impress on consciousness, which can addict their victims with their seductive partialities, ranging from religious faith to political commitment, and which thus carry with them not only the possibility of communal solidarity but also the ever present seeds of holocaustic or genocidal intent.[34]

Hence, it is because of her very wealth that the Goddess' is compelled to give birth to her child, consciousness, so that in the child she may come to know herself and in so doing complete both her life and that of the child. But here again her ambivalence is to be noted. For the birth of consciousness from her depths is never easy and rarely total. On her part she tends to keep the weaker ego for herself. Indeed, not infrequently such mother-bound consciousness, though always crippling and sometimes fatal, may not be wholly uncomfortable. How many moderns happily imprisoned in her social institutions, nationalist collectivities, or redemptive agencies thus live in the thrall of the Great or the Holy Mother willing always to give their lives in the defence of her Holy Land or cause in whatever form she demands? Though finally such life in the security of the collective womb turns to despair or anger because it conspires with the devouring mother to cheat life through the avoidance of the pain of becoming conscious, it is for many a continuing temptation. The psychological truncation or death Jung captures in this aspect of his psychology is especially evident when such attenuated development is presented by collective leaders in myriad lights as faith, ancestral loyalty, patriotism, civic duty, communal concern or any number of denials of the true self in the name of collective idolatry. In short, the devouring mother finds not a few all too willing to be eaten.

But even for those who achieve some degree of independent consciousness, the drama of Jung's mythology is not over. And here the dialectic at the heart of Jung's understanding of successful incest with the Goddess becomes most apparent. For even as she gives birth to an independent centre of consciousness, she remains always the source of its energy or libido. As pointed out above, to be so independent of her as to

---

34.   *Cf.* my ch. 6, "The Final Option: Mandalic Versus Holocaustic Faith," *The Illness That We Are: A Jungian Critique of Christianity* (Toronto: Inner City, 1984), p. 71f.

sever relations with her is the distinguishing feature and essence of patriarchal consciousness. Whether embodied in male or female, such consciousness is removed from its life-giving roots and so is all too often embroiled in the rapacious sterility and angry aggression in the name of reason and order, and sometimes even justice, which such uprootedness has spawned in our culture.

It is in the area of this dialectical relationship to the Goddess as the deepest dimension of the psyche that Jung's psychology can both identify the debilitating nature of patriarchal consciousness and point to strategies to undermine it. In this respect Jung could contribute to contemporary feminist thought and strategy by providing the resources for the corrosion of patriarchal consciousness while avoiding the "tar baby effect," understood as the difficulty of engaging patriarchalism without becoming part of it. Thus, if patriarchal consciousness were to be more widely understood in Jung's context as that state of consciousness which has a severed or attenuated connection with the unconscious, Jung's psychology could provide the much needed basis for a gender free understanding of patriarchalism. As such it could function to identify patriarchal consciousness wherever it occurred, even in such unlikely places as contemporary feminism, so often consciously devoted to its transformation.

This deeper appropriation of Jung's psychology would work to show that the connectedness of the ego to the energies of the Goddess through union with the intra-psychic contra-sexual works to vitalize, balance and extend the consciousness of both male and female. In terms of the male-female relationship Jung's psychology works, as it always does, first to differentiate and then to reunite the opposites within the individual. Consistent with this foundational theme of differentiation and reunification, Jung's psychology in the area of male-female relationship moves toward the goal of androgynous consciousness in both male and female psyche.

Androgyny, in a Jungian context, describes the native movement of the psyche to reunite the male or female ego, once they gain a modicum of conscious stability, with their opposite through a life-giving relationship to the inner contra-sexual, the anima in the male and the animus in the female. Androgynous consciousness, thus understood, is a substantial component of

Jung's understanding of the psyche's movement toward wholeness when this movement is focused through the male-female polarity. Put in the context of his psychology, his conception of androgyny renders false or in need of serious qualification such still to be heard statements as, "Androcentrism and misogyny distort Jung's discussions of women, the anima, the animus and the feminine."[35]

An integral understanding of Jung would furthermore negate the strange but still prevalent distortion of Jung's understanding of the animus as an exclusively negative power in the unconscious or, worse, as an ontological internalization and sacralization of male oppression.[36] Rather, the animus would be seen as Jung presents it, no doubt as an inner power which can and does betray and attack the feminine ego when he is in the possession of the negative mother, but also as the potential mediator of the sustaining powers of the Great Goddess in her benign face. As such the animus becomes a woman's greatest psycho-spiritual resource and fosters an autonomous individuality which alone insures that she will not become patriarchal in her response to patriarchalism.

Though Jung does indeed universalize and ontologize the living structures of the psyche, including the animus, there is nothing static or fixating about his ontology. Rather, it clearly depicts the archetypal structures of the unconscious, including the animus, as numinous powers, the bases of the Gods and Goddesses themselves, in organic conversation with the ego in their efforts to become incarnate in it in a process of mutual completion. To argue that such a concept of the animus sacralizes the male oppression of women in and of itself[37] is to deny the numinous power that in clinical experience shows itself so often and spontaneously in his manifestations in the female psyche. At a deeper level the proposed desacralization of the animus or of any other archetypal power fails to grasp

---

35. Demaris S. Wehr, *Jung and Feminism: Liberating Archetypes* (Boston: Beacon Press, 1987), pp. 65, 99.

36. *Ibid.*, p. 117f.

37. *Ibid.*, p. 124, for instance.

the foundational point of Jung's psychology of religion. Archetypal experience cannot be wholly desacralized because its impact on consciousness is the inner and only basis of humanity's experience of the sacred, a point obviously missed by those who wonder if humanity's sense of God, has an "external referent." This dynamic would include the impact, for better or worse, of the animus on female consciousness. For the male or female not to fear and respect such inner forces would remove the individual from the beginning of wisdom even as it divested such a victim of his or her deepest resource for self-affirmation, understood as an ever extending empathy supported ultimately by the Goddess' energies working through the anima or animus.[38]

In terms of the animus and patriarchy Jung's psychology would urge that a negative animus constellated in a woman through a patriarchal culture or environment can be most effectively overcome in the woman's recovery of a supportive animus as the basis both of her inner sense of worth and of her free and creative response to surrounding cultural pathology. Where this recovery of a sustaining animus is impaired or denied, it is difficult to see how a woman's response to patriarchy can avoid cloning it, since without the support of the animus her response must be limited to consciousness, and limitation to consciousness is the essence of the patriarchal. Thus little is to be gained in either the denial of the reality of the animus or in the misrepresentation of Jung's understanding of the animus as an always negative power. Such a strategy would be like denying the existence or need of the heart as the best response to a coronary.

Jung's ontologizing and divinizing of the energies of anima and animus is thus not oppressive to either male or female but simply a portrayal of the ground movement of the psyche towards a wholeness in which the energies of the Great Mother are mediated to the male through the inner female and to the female through the inner male. In both male and female the relationship to these inner powers can go awry, especially in that state Jung calls motherboundedness. It produces in the male the *puer*, the little boy, whose consciousness never significantly moves beyond the psychic

---

[38]   *Ibid.*, p. 110f, for a discussion of the anima and "fear" of women.

womb. Much of Jung's psychology is a critique of this condition in the male, which makes it difficult if not impossible to contend that his psychology is more favourable to the male or more critical of the feminine. Its basic problematic is puerility in male or female. Where it is specifically directed at the female, Jung is describing the process of motherboundedness, usually through the coalition of the negative animus and negative mother complexes, in a specifically feminine configuration. To deny that women too can become victims of a negative mother working through a vitiating animus is unreal and defies clinical experience. To argue that Jung is biased in his depiction of this condition is to deny that it can and does happen in amazing agreement with just how Jung describes it. Naivete in denying the hazards and not infrequent casualties of feminine individuation which Jung describes simply becomes a form of the ideological denial of recurring pathological possibilities in the feminine. In certain circles such denial seems currently to be moving toward the second phase of the Immaculate Deception.

Indeed, in the response to the suffering inflicted by a patriarchal culture, the societal spread of an increasingly conscious relationship to the animus as mediator of a new feminine self-confidence and self-valuation is the most powerful contribution to the creation of a mythical alternative to the current patriarchal consciousness that the modern women might offer. Paradoxically, where the animus is not operative as the link with the Goddess as the author of the new, the attendant consciousness in the female psyche would disqualify itself as a significant contributor to a mythical alternative to patriarchalism. Thus, any feminist strategy against the patriarchal which would unequivocally denigrate Jung's conception of the animus would effectively serve to remove the woman from the support of the animus acting in the service of whatever revelation the Goddess might currently be proposing as a living option to still reigning patriarchal mythology. Such strategy guarantees the victory of patriarchalism and the defeat of feminist aspirations where these aspirations are more than simply extending the patriarchal to wider circles of women.

One sometimes suspects that such self-defeating strategies are grounded on a surreptitious and insidious envy of patriarchal consciousness, which functions then to appropriate patriarchal consciousness for women rather than working to undermine it on a cultural basis as it effects both sexes. If this is the case, then feminism might well have to go through a period of "successful" appropriation of patriarchal consciousness in the pursuit of "equality" in patriarchal prerogatives. This would mean that the modern feminine soul may have to suffer fully the poverty of patriarchal consciousness and spirituality, hopefully to be led eventually, through its own attainment of a certain parity of patriarchal depression, to align itself with male victims of the same blight in the search for a newer myth.

Thus contemporaneity may be faced with two stages in the development of the feminine response to the patriarchal. In the first the goal is to achieve equality or parity. Where this is a matter of simple justice and dignity, one can hardly deny its validity. But if it means nothing more than the extension to women of patriarchal consciousness and its rewards, it may, through the depression and sense of spiritual impoverishment that attaches to such consciousness, lead both men and women to a second stage, the search for a more humanizing social and cultural mythology to which Jung's conception of androgyny could make a significant contribution.

For it can hardly be denied that the suffering informing much of feminist consciousness is a suffering that is real, culturally widespread and harmful to both sexes. If the potential value of this suffering is examined in the light of Jung's understanding of the compensation offered by the unconscious to cultural pathology as revelation, then the suffering of the contemporary feminine spirit or soul could become a significant factor in the emergence of a true alternative to patriarchy. But this alternative would itself have to have the power and status of a myth to be truly corrosive of its patriarchal precedent. If a one-sided and so pathologizing deification of the powers of consciousness, often in alliance with a rapacious technology, is of the essence of the patriarchal myth as the ground of Christian religiosity, then its true compensation and removal would itself require nothing less than a new religious or mythical consciousness. The feminist movement could make a significant contribution to this new consciousness, not by removing itself from the unconscious as source of the sought for revelation, but by allowing its suffering to become the occasion for the surfacing from the unconscious of a true alternative, operating eventually with the force of a new revelation. Just as Tillich writes that only a symbol can replace a symbol, Jung might add that only an archetype can transform a stereotype and so corrode the current patriarchal congealment in the surfacing of a new myth. In the end, for those who suffer under patriarchy only a new myth, a new revelation, will suffice. Needless to say, it is not likely to be provided by patriarchy in either its male or female forms, since the distinguishing feature of such consciousness is removal from the unconscious as the source of all revelation, including the one now sought as superceding patriarchalism.

Turning now from the social to the personal implications of the Great Mother or Goddess, one might argue with considerable justification that the relation of the ego to the power of the mother complex, in the extended sense Jung gives it, is *the* most important of the dynamics operative in the psyche. The primacy of this force in the psyche is of great import in the discussion of patriarchal uprootedness, understood as unawareness of her being and power. This is because of the ambivalent intent toward consciousness which Jung identified in this energy at the basis of psychic life.

In his experience, such patriarchal ignorance of her presence and power becomes the occasion of her exercising her darker side. She can do this in innumerable ways, but on examination, they usually reduce to variations of disabling or destroying the conscious centre of the personality by divesting it of its shadow power and/or severing the connection of consciousness with the contra-sexual as the bearer of life's deeper energies. For instance, in a frequently played scenario, if she can strip her child, the ego, mesmerized by the illusory self-image of being an agent of pure and benevolent reason, of its shadow power in the form of all personal traits repulsive to Mother, Mother is then freed to marry the disarmed victim to Mother's choice. Mother's choice is hand-picked to fail the hapless lover by removing the support and creative energy that only the relation to the positive animus or anima and its reflection in the external lover can provide. Deprived of the strength and autonomy of viewpont the shadow might supply and divested of an internal spouse and external support, the naive agent of pure light, male or female, becomes another morsel for the devouring mother's insatiable appetite.[39]

Thus consciousness as it gains a relative independence over against the Goddess must continue to deal with her, always in the interests of receiving the grace of her energies and not infrequently in contesting with her for a fuller conscious personality and more adequate relationality. In either case, re-entering the womb, incest with the Great Mother, becomes a universal psycho-spiritual necessity.[40] The only option is whether such incest is done consciously and voluntarily or whether neglect of the Goddess forces the issue - usually in a much more painful series of events. Jung captures the universality and necessity of this incestuous re-immersion in the maternal origins when he writes, "This is as much as to say that anyone who is destined to descend into a deep pit had better set about it with all the necessary precautions rather than risk falling into the hole backwards."[41]

It is in the context of the universal demand of incestuous renewal that Jung locates in his mythology the theme of suffering. He implies that the return to the Goddess, re-entering the womb, is rarely undertaken unless suffering forces it. Indeed, it is most frequently the pain of the conflict between her legitimate, compelling, but totally opposing truths suffered to the death which occasions the re-immersion in her, there to find the unifying symbol which bears to consciousness the energies and more embracing empathy of resurrected life.[42]

In a slightly different imagery describing the same process, Jung points to the fight with the dragon,[43] perhaps most familiar to us in the myth

[39]. C. G. Jung, "The Dual Mother," *Symbols of Transformation*, CW 5, pars. 465, 466, pp. 307, 308.

[40]. C. G. Jung, "The Battle for Deliverance from the Mother," *Symbols of Transformation*, CW 5, par. 450, p. 294.

[41]. C. G. Jung, "Christ, A Symbol of the Self," CW 9ii, par. 125, p. 70.

[42]. This explains Jung's fondness for the image of the Christ figure dying between the opposites of a Yes and No spoken by a "good" and "bad" thief who die with him. *Cf.* "Answer to Job," CW 11, par. 659, p. 417 and par. 739, p. 455.

[43]. *Cf. Symbols of Transformation*, CW 5, fn. 110, pp. 362, 363.

of St. George, and the night sea journey taken from Egyptian and other religions.[44] In the latter imagery the dialectic gives more emphasis to the cyclical nature of the process, the entry into and out of the unconscious, and to the role of the ego as in some sense a hero or heroine. Let us caution that describing the ego as hero or heroine is a legitimate use of language in a Jungian context only as long as one clearly realizes that such a hero or heroine is a thoroughly tattered and battered one. Such a protagonist enters or, more frequently, is dragged into the realm of the Goddess to confront her and to demand or beg from her her treasure. The content of the recovery of the pearl of great price can be described clinically as all that had been denied to the suffering consciousness forced to plead with her for its painfully absent wholeness. For a full catalogue of what can be denied and needs to be recovered, I would refer the interested to Grimm's fairy tales or to the fairy tales of the culture of one's choice.

Needless to say, such vigorous confrontation with the immensely superior forces of the Goddess does wonders for strengthening the ego, male or female. Nor is it surprising that the Goddess thus challenged or petitioned usually does yield up her treasure and in the twinkling of an eye or the sounding of a trumpet changes from the dragon to the fairy godmother, betraying her secret that both faces are really two sides of her one powerful truth. In pondering the ambivalence and shape-shifting so central to the role of the Goddess in Jung's myth, one has the impression that he thought her ultimately benign. One suspects she welcomes the challenge of those who dare enter her domain, harrowing though such entry be, and that she is only too eager to yield her wealth to those who force themselves upon her because in their return to consciousness she is herself completed.

Thus speculation on the Goddess and on her ultimately benign intent toward consciousness is of some importance. For it should be obvious that Jung's psychology, grounded as it is on the mythology of the Goddess, can just as easily become a world view with profound philosophical, religious, and theological consequences. When it is thus addressed, Jung's psychology clearly raises the question of the ultimate intent and the nature of the

---

44. *Ibid.*, par. 308, p. 210f.

64

Goddess. This question becomes the functional equivalent of the metaphysical and theological questions of the goodness of creation, of the nature of the ground which seeks expression in it, and of the direction, if any, in which consciousness is moved by its creative precedent. Should humanity become widely convinced that the answer to these questions are fundamentally negative, the search for the joy of life which makes the present tolerable and the future possible might be called off, as Teilhard de Chardin warned.[45] His abiding fear was that the end might come through the cold of universal depression before the failure of the sun's sustaining light.

Whatever the answer to these deeper questions may be, the proper understanding and appropriation of the cyclical movement of the ego's love affair with the Great Goddess, its movement into and out of her, is of crucial importance to Jung. Our individual and collective survival and welfare depend upon it, because it is from such intercourse that we derive the will to live, informed by an ever expanding empathy. It is obvious that Jung's psychology eliminates two pathologizing extremes in this cycle. The first extreme is the refusal to re-enter the womb. This refusal is the substance of patriarchal pathology described above, the fate of the starving, depressed or outraged prisoner of consciousness. The second extreme is refusal or inability to return to the conscious world with the recreational energies given by the Goddess. This is the fate of the addict and the truth of the mystic. The former can get in but not out. The latter can do both. Jung writes of such enticing danger faced by addict and mystic alike when he refers to the temptation to "...wed onself to the abyss and blot out all memory in its embrace."[46] He clearly links the addictive possibility to the mystical experience when he adds, "This piece of mysticism is innate in all better men as the 'longing for the mother,' the nostalgia for the source from which we came."[47]

45. *Cf.* for example, "The Contingence of the Universe and Man's Zest for Survival," *Christianity and Evolution*, trans. Rene Hague (London: Collins, 1971), p. 221f.

46. C. G. Jung, *Two Essays on Analytical Psychology*, CW 7, par. 261.

47. *Ibid.*

For Jung the achievement of psychic maturity is never free of agony. On the one hand, the sufferer is driven to forego the comfortable certitudes of a perspective, often gained with considerable pain. On the other hand, consciousness, once immersed in its transforming origin, must resist the temptation to give itself forever to her enticing dissolution. Yet, when successful incest with the Mother, entrance into her recreating depths and return to consciousness, becomes the rhythm of any life, that life, in Jung's experience, constantly dies in its conflicted and restricted consciousness toward patterns of resolution of opposites and broader, more encompassing empathies, in a process that can never be completed in a lifetime but can never be avoided without the sin of self-betrayal. In this reciprocity the individual is redeemed through the ingression into the Goddess, and the Goddess is redeemed when her powerful oppositions are reconciled in the consciousness she first dissolves in order thus to enrich, unify and extend.

Especially in his appreciation of the mystics as those adventurous souls whose experience of the archetypal world of the Goddess is more immediate than most does Jung point to material which makes her a more imposing psycho-spiritual power than even his own psychology can easily handle. For instance, the writings of Mecthilde of Magdeburg[48] and Hadewijch of Antwerp,[49] two thirteenth-century expressions of the mystical marriage tradition, illustrate the further reaches of the Goddess as experienced by women. Both depict orgasmic unity with their divine lover and animus, a youthful Christ figure, as but a preliminary step to a total loss of identity in that power which precedes even the lingering duality suggested in the imagery and experience of love-making. It is from this total loss of identity in the Goddess as the wholly undifferentiated source of all that is that they return to consciousness and to their culture with a renewed and expanded awareness empowering them to give to that culture the

---

48.   *Cf.* my "Love, Celibacy and the Inner Marriage" in *Love, Celibacy and the Inner Marriage* (Toronto: Inner City, 1987), p. 25f.

49.   *Cf.* in particular "Visions" in *Hadewijch, the Complete Works,* Classics of Western Spirituality (New York: Paulist Press, 1980), p. 259f.

rejuvenation and critique which their experience of dissolution in the matrix of all reality has given to them.

In the following century Meister Eckhart's writings witness the same rhythm in a male experience. A fuller discussion of his contribution follows in the next chapter. Put briefly in the context of a discussion of Jung's understanding of the Great Mother, Eckhart described the fruit of intercourse with the deeper unconscious in the imagery of the birth of God or of the Son in the soul as an experience preliminary to the breakthrough into a unity with God so intense that all differences between the divine and the human fuse into an invigorating nothingness.[50]   Such experience of dissolution drives Eckhart to the statement, "I pray to God to rid me of God...,"[51] that is, of all differentiation between his being and that of God. Worked out theologically, it drives him clearly to distinguish between the highly defined and active male Trinity and the Godhead which precedes it. This Godhead rests in itself and yet is clearly the source of all differentiation, including that of the Trinity.   Though Eckhart lacked the psychological awareness and conceptual equipment so to formulate it, from Jung's perspective he had experienced the ultimate truth of the Goddess whom Eckhart calls the Godhead but who is obviously in his experience herself the mother of the Trinity.

Again, from such dissolution in the Goddess' deepest nature, Eckhart found the courage and energy to grace Christendom with his being rejected as a heretic and so to bear early witness to the peculiar psycho-spiritual situation the Christian world is in, namely, that the recovery of our current health lies in the recovery of our past heresy. For in Eckhart's trial it became obvious that the Christian collective could tolerate neither the natural intimacy of the Goddess to the psyche as its depth dimension, nor the

---

50.   *Cf.* an excellent treatment of these distinct movements of birth and breakthrough in Eckhart in John D. Caputo, *The Mystical Element in Heidegger's Thought* (Athens, Ohio: Ohio University Press, 1984), Section Three, p. 97f.

51.   Meister Eckhart, sermon, "Blessed Are the Poor" from *Meister Eckhart*, translation and commentary by Reiner Schurmann (Bloomington: Indiana University Press, 1977), pp. 216, 219.

challenge of the radical nature of her dissolving and renewing powers, nor her precedence to and generation of the still reigning male triad.[52]

In conclusion, let us describe some of the consequences of Jung's recovery of the Goddess in our contemporary situation. Jung's identification of the Goddess as the deepest dimension of the psyche grounds his indictment of our society. Culturally we are an uprooted people because we have lost living touch with her vivifying and unifying energies. His understanding of the Goddess further provides the basis of an appreciative undermining of our still prevailing religious myths, based as they are on transcendent, wholly other, male, one and only Gods, of whom there are currently at least three in contention reaching out from the west end of the Mediterranean. The Goddess can appreciate these contending male *monotheoi* because she is herself their mother. But there is an undermining element currently operative in her wisdom, for the Goddess knows also that the time of their dissolution is at hand. It is at hand for the most obvious reason that our common humanity is collectively threatened by the hatred and bloodshed unleashed whenever the communities formed under the projection of these one and only contending Gods meet geographically. But it is at hand for a deeper evolutionary reason grounded in the development of human psycho-spirituality. This reason is based on the slowly dawning realization that the origin of lesser Gods and Goddesses is the great Goddess herself and that she dwells in the depths of the psyche of each individual and of humanity universally. No doubt she has given humanity a valuable gift in her creation of masculine deities. For some millennia they have shown us what lies within us and provided the kind of restraint needed to make our current civilizations possible. Thus we can be thankful to her for their creation even as she currently leads us to the wisdom that they are no longer tolerable.

As the male *monotheoi* are dissolved through the dissolution of the projections which created them and the consequence of their dissolution is

---

52.   For the bull of condemnation, "In Agrico Dominico," *cf. Meister Eckhart*, translation and introduction by Edmund Colledge, O. S. A., and Bernard McGinn (New York: Paulist Press, 1981), p. 77f.

pursued in any depth, humanity, individually and collectively, will have to face the power of the Great Goddess as their mother and generator, this time more consciously aware of what it is doing and who it is facing. If the Great Goddess can be thus consciously accessed, Jung would understand her to proffer to our contemporary humanity the resolution of its conflicts through their dissolution in her creative depths towards a consciousness which could better approximate her universal embrace. For one cannot return to consciousness from dissolution and recreation in the Great Mother without bringing something of her universal sympathy to a world on the brink of eliminating consciousness entirely in unquestioning religious obedience to lesser Gods and Goddesses in political or religious face and sometimes in both. In the final analysis, the most significant aspect of Jung's recovery of the Goddess is the contribution it may make to that now crucial strategy for the loss of our current faiths in the interest first of the survival and then of the enrichment of our common humanity.

Let us turn to a more detailed examination of the religious experience of a man whom Jung obviously admired and frequently cited, in no small part because of the fact that Eckhart's union with the abyss dimension of the psyche was as total as his consequent universal affirmation of the sacredness of all being which such immersion sponsored in him upon his return from it. Meister Eckhart is but one of many mystics cited extensively by Jung, but his experience of the nether dimension of the psyche was so profound that it serves well to illustrate the majesty, the power and perhaps even the terrible yet ultimately benign nature of the Goddess who precedes the Trinity, herself the formless and resting might from whom all form and life derive.

CHAPTER THREE

JUNG AND ECKHART:
BREAKTHROUGH TO THE GODDESS

Exploring the affinity of Eckhart's religious experience with Jung's experience of the psyche can work a valuable and reciprocal illumination of the truth each has to offer. Jung can give to Eckhart's experience the modern psychological insight that Eckhart formally lacked. Thus a Jungian hermeneutic of Eckhart's experience could show that it is an experience of the furthest reach of the psyche, where consciousness loses itself in an unqualified return to its source in the interests of its renewal and eventual expansion. On the other hand, Eckhart's experience might reveal to a Jungian perspective that there are reaches of the psyche which in some sense actually precede or outstrip even the unrealized latency or potentiality for conscious expression that Jung identified in the archetypal powers of the collective unconscious.

A major difficulty in amplifying the affinity between the spirit and works of Carl Jung and of Meister Eckhart is the apparent removal from current "practical" concerns and life, psychological, religious or social, which the exploration of such a connection would seem to entail. Whatever justification might exist for such an unlikely endeavour in today's climate comes in large part from Jung himself. For, in the final analysis, it is the latter's demonstrable interest in Eckhart which provides whatever dubious warrant exists for an examination of the spiritual affinity between them.

70

Though the effort of addressing the link between Jung's psychology and Eckhart's religious experience is demanding, its yield might be of great value to the worlds of Theology, Philosophy, Religious Studies, Spirituality and Psychology, to name but a few. Such conversation would engage all of these areas of the human spirit without forcing one upon the other or giving to one perspective an imperial dominance. The conversation between Eckhart and Jung might thus be expected to yield much wealth, because such conversation could work to make evident the reality of the renewing and energizing depths of the psyche as a universally available resource, experienced no doubt in a surpassing manner by Eckhart himself, but there for all, whether accessed religiously, psychologically or in some other mode. In this manner the value of Eckhart's experience could be accessed by those to whom these depths are no longer available through a formally religious approach but whose lives stand in as great a need of reinvigoration by them as was Eckhart's and as is every life seeking its full vitality.

It is not difficult to prove that Jung was an admirer of Eckhart. Throughout his *Collected Works* and the two volumes of his letters, Jung cites Eckhart 38 times from 21 widely varying loci in the early twentieth-century, two-volumes translation by C. de B. Evans[1] of Franz Pfeiffer's nineteenth-century collection of Eckhart's German works.[2] Perhaps in an even more telling manner, Jung cites Eckhart twice in his late autobiography *Memories, Dream and Reflections*. In the first citation Jung pays tribute to Eckhart as the source of youthful inspiration in matters religious and philosophical. He writes, "only in Meister Eckhart did I feel the breath of life..." and then adds, probably out of a tribute to the limitations of his early scholarly pretensions, "...not that I understood him."[3] In the second citation Jung refers to Eckhart in the context of a concern which became increasingly central to the maturing Jung. In this reference to Eckhart, whom he here associates with Joachim di Fiore and Jacob Boehme, Jung characterizes him as a peripheral figure in

1. Franz Pfeiffer, *Meister Eckhart*, 2 vols., trans. C. de B. Evans (London: John M. Watkins, 1924).
2. Franz Pfeiffer, *Meister Eckhart: Predigten und Traktate* (Leipzig: Aalen, 1857).
3. C. G. Jung, *Memories, Dreams, Reflections* (New York: Random House, 1961), pp. 68-69.

Western theology and spirituality whose rejected experience contributed greatly to the lack of spiritual maturation of the Christian myth in its historical unfolding and so to its current sterility.[4]

That Jung was not a casual reader of Eckhart is evident in the breadth of citations Jung selects from the roughly six-hundred-page Evans translation on which Jung relied in his *Collected Works*. Moreover, one has the impression after a personal reading of the Evans translation that Jung almost uncannily perceived in the Eckhart corpus expressions of the movement of the deeper psyche that only someone with Jung's sensitivity to the unconscious could so readily and quickly extract from such a mass of material. In Jung's appropriation of Eckhart it quickly becomes obvious that like spirit is responding to like spirit.

Behind the frequency of Jung's citation of Eckhart, one suspects that deeper issues lie. For Jung seems to interpret Eckhart out of a wider position which emerges when Jung's statements on mysticism itself are read organically in the context of their appearance throughout the *Collected Works*. Read in this manner, Jung must be understood to hold that the mystics experience the numinosity of the archetypal world without mediation and so with that intensity of experience which gives rise to religion personally and collectively or institutionally throughout humanity's history. Thus, he will describe mystics as "...people who have had a particularly vivid experience of the processes of the unconscious. Mystical experience is experience of the archetypes."[5] This means that from a Jungian perspective the study of mystical experience becomes at the same time the study of the deeper movements of the psyche, which themselves are the source of humanity's ineradicable religious impulse and its expression.

But this characteristically Jungian perspective carries with it a two-sided hermeneutic. On the one hand, Jungian categories can illuminate mystical experience by showing it to be grounded in and expressive of the deepest movements of the psyche. In so doing, Jung performs a valuable service to the contemporary world. He shows the inescapability of the

---

4.   *Ibid.*, p. 332.

5.   "The Tavistock Lectures," CW 18, par. 218, p. 5.

72

religious sentiment, grounded as it is in the nature of the psyche and so in human nature. In this manner he makes such experience psychologically available even to the religiously dispossessed and institutionally disenchanted modern by showing not only its life-giving value but its accessibility in the psyche universally and naturally.

However, the other side of Jung's hermeneutic applied to an examination of mystical experience could be threatening to certain too shallow models of the psyche still operative in contemporary psychology in both its theoretical and therapeutic faces. For understood as a manifestation of the ground movements of the psyche, mystical experience can reveal to the psychologist dimensions of the psyche which, though they remain universal human propensities, can with difficulty be included in existing paradigms or models of psychic life and maturity. In this sense the psychological understanding of mystical experience can broaden and deepen the understanding of the psyche itself and so force the psychologist to rethink and expand current models of the psyche, especially those which would constrict the psyche to its relatively small conscious or rational component. Needless to say, an exploration of those levels of psychic reality which precede and give rise to consciousness would, from Jung's viewpoint, lead necessarily and naturally into the religion-generating propensities, the archetypes, native to the deeper psyche. In this manner the investigation would itself take on a religious coloration.

In the interface of Jung and Eckhart, both sides of this process seem to be operative. Jung uses Eckhart and other mystics to confirm and to illustrate his understanding of the deeper movements of psychic life. As suggested, in doing this he shows to modernity its continued psychic affinity with the profound religious experiences of the past even in a religionless culture. But Eckhart, speaking in a religious and theological idiom, may also point to depths of the psyche which Jung, in his admiration of Eckhart obviously could appreciate, but with difficulty integrate fully into his model of the psyche. At the heart of the interface of Jung and Eckhart we come to see what Jung's psychology reveals about the human soul and its movements through Jung's appreciation of mystical experience. But at the same time mysticism, and especially Eckhart's mysticism, can reveal even to Jung the possibility of a deeper stratum of the psyche which may evade and in some sense extend the model of the psyche Jung has left us in both its theoretical and therapeutic implications. This latter possibility is opened up through the radical understanding of dissolution in the Godhead central to Eckhart's experience and no doubt understood and appreciated by Jung, even though it may point to a dimension of psyche preceding even the archetypal. This point will be elaborated below.

At a level of discussion prior to the relative depth of the psyche into which Jung and Eckhart may have respectively entered, it remains true that both men, separated by six centuries, felt that the movement into one's divine depths was the basis of the recovery of one's balance, of one's energies for life and of one's extended empathies. For this reason the mining of these depths in the light that both Eckhart and Jung cast upon them could be of immense, though admittedly indirect, meaning for a spiritually uprooted and so exhausted contemporary world.

In what follows I would like briefly to present a sketch of Eckhart's life, because a rudimentary knowledge of his biography is essential in tracing the development and shifts in his thought and work. Then I would like to expose the three major areas in the *Collected Works* where Jung relies heavily on Eckhart, give a brief summary of the major distinctive positions in Eckhart's work, and end by drawing conclusions from the comparison of his work with Jung's.

First, let us put Eckhart in historical perspective. He was born in the German province of Thuringia around 1260 in one of two towns called Hockheim, one near Erfurt, and one near Gotha. Historians remain divided on which Hockheim it was.[6] Opinion favouring Erfurt can draw support from the fact that Eckhart there entered the Dominican novitiate in his mid-

---

6.   E. Colledge, "Historical Data," *Meister Eckhart* (New York: Paulist Press, 1981), p. 5, states he could have been born in either Hockheim. Armand E. Maurer, *Master Eckhart Parisian Questions and Prologues* (Toronto: Pontifical Institute of Mediaeval Studies, 1974), p. 9, refers to "...one of two towns named Hockheim." James M. Clark, *Meister Eckhart: An Introduction to the Study of His Works with An Anthology of His Sermons* (London: Thomas Nelson and Sons Ltd., 1957), p. 11, favours Gotha and cites H. S. Denifle as his source, *Archive fur die Literatur und Kirkengeschicte des Mittelalters* (Berlin and Freiburg), pp. 349-356. J. Ancelet-Hustache also favours Gotha, *Master Eckhart and the Rhineland Mystics*, trans. Hilda Graef (New York: Harper Torchbooks, 1957), p. 23.

74

teens. At the age of seventeen he can be located as a student of Arts and a Dominican studying at the University of Paris.[7] Thus it is apparent that it did not take long for the order to recognize his academic capacities. He continued his studies in Cologne in 1280, possibly under or influenced by Albert the Great,[8] Aquinas' teacher, thought by Jung to have been imbued with the spirit of alchemy.[9] In 1293-94 Eckhart was back in Paris lecturing on the *Sentences* of Peter Lombard, a requirement then for the Master's degree.

At this point in his career, a second major capacity, that of the administrator, becomes apparent. Sometime prior to 1300 he was named Prior of the Dominican house in Erfurt and Vicar-Provincial of Thuringia. Later in 1303 he was to become a major superior or administrator as provincial of the province of Saxony, and in 1307 was offered a second major province. Thus his academic career was mixed with a marked capacity for administration. This is worthy of note in allaying the misconception that those whose experience is as deep as Eckhart's are somehow withdrawn from life and its demands. It simply is not true in Eckhart's life nor in the lives of authentic mystics.

In 1302 he received the degree of Master of Theology from Paris University and taught there for a first period until 1303, to be followed after his administrative period with a second period in Paris from 1311-1313. During his periods of teaching, Eckhart authored tracts on various theological subjects written in the best of scholastic Latin and using the very formal mode of argumentation that attached to scholasticism. Though many

---

[7.] Colledge, *op. cit.,* p. 7. Colledge cites J. Koch, "Kritische Studien zum Leben Meister Eckharts," *Kleine Schriften*, vol. 2, p. 249.

[8.] *Cf.* T. Kaeppe, "Praedicator monoculus. Sermons parisiens de la fin du XII siècle," *Archivum Fratrum Praedicatorum*, 27 (1957), pp. 120-167. *Cf.* also E. Colledge, *op. cit.,* pp. 5, 6, where Colledge argues Kosch also believed Albert to have taught Eckhart in Cologne.

[9.] *Cf.* C. G. Jung, "The Sign of the Fishes," CW 9ii, par. 143, p. 87, where Jung links the Holy Ghost movement with Albertus Magnus, strangely with Aquinas himself, Roger Bacon, and Meister Eckhart. *Cf.* also "Letter to Pere Bruno," CW 18, par. 1530, p. 678, where Jung again connects Albert the Great with the spirit of the times and so with alchemy. In our opinion, Roger Bacon and Aquinas are strange members to include in alchemical sensitivity. It would appear that the Spirit movement and its representatives like Joachim di Fiore, Francis of Assisi and Eckhart are possessed of affinities whose absence in Aquinas and Bacon are characteristic of their positions and forerunner of the split between science and depth experience.

of the propositions that were to be later condemned were extracts from his Latin tracts, it was not really until he began yet a third career as a distinguished preacher preaching in the vernacular in Germany that questions of his orthodoxy began to surface.

The transition followed his transfer to the Dominican house in Strassbourg in 1314, where he began to combine the roles of preaching with teaching. In the final analysis, it appears to have been his preaching rather than his teaching which eventually made him famous or infamous, depending on one's theological tastes, and which led him to his confrontation with the Inquisition. Shortly after he moved to the Dominican house of studies in Cologne, his preaching to lay people and to communities of sisters drew the attention of the Franciscan Archbishop of Cologne, a noted heresy hunter, Henry of Virnberg. In 1326 Henry sponsored an initial heresy trial, after a fellow Dominican acting in the role of a papal investigator had cleared Eckhart. In 1326 Eckhart defended himself against various lists of statements of questionable orthodoxy extracted from both his Latin and German works. Early in 1327 Eckhart denied the canonicity, that is, the ecclesial legality, of the proceedings against him in Cologne and appealed to the Apostolic See, the papacy, then resident in Avignon. In February 1327 he defended himself publicly in the Dominican church in Cologne and some time after left for Avignon to have his case heard there.

Some time between his departure for Avignon after February 13, 1327 and before April 30, 1328, he died at a place unknown, while his trial was in process. The latter date is fixed in a letter sent by Pope John XX to Henry, the Archbishop of Cologne, assuring him that Eckhart's trial was continuing after the latter's death.[10] On March 27, 1329, the bull of condemnation "In agrico dominico" lists 28 propositions of which 17 are described as heresy and 11 are suspect, though capable of bearing an orthodox meaning with proper interpretation.[11] The bull mentions that Eckhart had retracted prior to death all error attached to the propositions. Thus a man who believed

[10]   Bernard McGinn, "Eckhart's Condemnation Reconsidered," *The Thomist*, vol. 44, 1980, p. 397.

[11]   *Cf.* for a translation of the bull of condemnation "Documents Relating to Eckhart's Condemnation," in *Meister Eckhart* (New York: Paulist Press, 1981), p. 71f.

76

himself to be an obedient son of the Church and had served it well as theologian, preacher and administrator died during an investigation into his orthodoxy, leaving the work of a lifetime and his reputation under a cloud of suspicion.

In the wake of his condemnation, Eckhart became a peripheral figure for five to six centuries.[12] His disciples Johann Tauler (1300-1361) and Heinrich Suso (1300-1366) tried to keep alive a moderate or orthodox version of his views. Luther read Tauler and may have read Eckhart in Tauler's work.[13] Only in the nineteenth century in German romanticism and idealism did Eckhart enjoy a certain revival. Franz Baader introduced him to Hegel, who mentions him in his *Philosophy of Religion*.[14] With Pfeiffer's nineteenth-century publication of his German works, fresh dispute erupted over his orthodoxy.[15] Many pointed to an undeniable pantheism at the core of his thought and to an over emphasis on a symbolic understanding of religious truths. Other especially nineteenth-century neo-Thomists such as H. S. Denifle,[16] encouraged by the later recovery of Eckhart's more formal and allegedly more orthodox Latin manuscripts, tried to depict him as both orthodox and Aristotelian. Modern scholarship would deny the latter and at least question the former. His distance from an Artistotelian and so Thomistic spirit or world view is made obvious by contemporary scholarly

---

12.   For an account of the fate of Eckhart's work in the period immediately following his death, *cf*. Ancelet-Hustache, "Rhineland Mysticism after Master Eckhart," *op. cit.*, pp. 139-178.

13.   *Cf*. Steven Ozment, "Eckhart and Luther: German Mysticism and Protestantism," *The Thomist*, vol. 42, 1978, p. 260. *Cf*. also Colledge, *op. cit.*, p. 16.

14.   *Cf*. Ancelet-Hustache, *op. cit.*, pp. 172-173; James M. Clark, *The Great German Mystics: Eckhart, Tauler, and Suso* (New York: Russell and Russell, 1949), p. 27.

15.   For a discussion of the development of 19th-century Eckhart scholarship after Pfeiffer, *cf*. Clark, *op. cit.*, pp. 27-35.

16.   *Cf*. accounts of the Dominican Aristotelian effort to lead Eckhart back into the fold in James M. Clark and John V. Skinner, *Treatises and Sermons of Meister Eckhart* (New York: Octagon Books, 1983), p. 16; James M. Clark, *The Great German Mystics: Eckhart, Tauler, and Suso* (New York: Russell and Russell, 1970), pp. 30-32; Ancelet-Hustache, *Master Eckhart and The Rhineland Mystics*, trans. Hilda Graef (New York: Harper Torchbooks, 1957), p. 174.

explorations of Eckhart's connections with Heidegger's mysticism and the Zen tradition.[17]

This is the man to whom Jung attributes a premonitory experience of what Jung came to term the self six hundred years before his culture could bring it to the more precise conscious expression it was to receive in Jung's psychology and in other cultural expressions in the nineteenth and twentieth centuries. Of this side of Eckhart's truth Jung writes, "Only in the nineteenth century did he find a public at all capable of appreciating the grandeur of his mind."[18] This is the man to whom Jung admits an indebtedness for two of the most basic psycho-spiritual elements in his own psychology, namely, the valuing of the capacity to "let be" and the realization that suffering is the fastest way to maturity. Thus Jung pays tribute to Eckhart for giving to him his appreciation and practice of that "letting go," which in traditional religious language is termed "resignation," and in a more Heideggerian idiom "releasement," rooted in the German word "gelazenheit." With both Jung and Eckhart, and possibly Heidegger, the term came to refer to a certain renewing passivity allowing the powers of God or psyche or being which infinitely transcend the ego as its native background to work their renewal from beyond time and space on a consciousness solidly grounded within the confines of finitude.[19] Perhaps as a complement to this esoteric side of his spirituality, Jung pays frequent tribute to Eckhart for the theme Eckhart repeats throughout his work, namely, that suffering is the swiftest way to perfection even when that suffering takes the form of moral failure.[20] In this

---

17.   For Eckhart's relation to Heidegger, *cf.* John D. Caputo, *The Mystical Element in Heidegger's Thought* (Athens, Ohio: Ohio University Press, 1978) and Caputo's "Fundamental Themes in Meister Eckhart's Mysticism," *The Thomist*, vol. 42, 1978, p. 197f. For Eckhart's relation to Zen, *cf.* Reiner Schurmann, *Meister Eckhart, Mystic and Philosopher* (Bloomington: Indiana University Press, 1978) and Schurmann's "The Loss of Origin in Soto Zen and In Meister Eckhart," *The Thomist,* vol. 42, 1978, p. 281f.

18.   C. G. Jung, "Gnostic Symbols of the Self," CW 9ii, par. 302, p. 194.

19.   C. G. Jung, CW 13, par. 20, p. 16; CW 14, par. 258, p. 201.

20.   C. G. Jung *Letters,* 2 vols., ed. Gerhard Adler and Aniela Jaffe (Princeton: Princeton University Press, 1975), vol. 2, anonymous letter, April 28, 1955, p. 248, and anonymous letter, June 29, 1965, p. 311. *Cf.* also CW 6, par. 411, 415, pp. 242, 245. Both letters cite Eckhart's phrase that suffering is "...the swiftest steed that bears you to perfection." The citations from CW 6 imply that part of the suffering is moral failure.

dimension of Eckhart, Jung saw a precedent to his psychology of the shadow, whose appearance in the form of apparent moral defeat can be the beginning of the individual's psychic redemption.

These are some of the ground themes in Eckhart that attracted Jung to his spirit, but there are three places throughout Jung's work in which his indebtedness to Eckhart is peculiarly evident. In volume six, he uses Eckhart to illustrate his understanding of the relativity of God and to help in his formulation of the flow of psychic energies within the psyche. In volume nine ii, he associates Eckhart with gnostic thought. In volume eleven, he relates Eckhart to Zen in the context of the individual's immediate and imageless access to the ground of truth and life, the matrix of consciousness itself, the unimaged ground of all imagery.

An examination of Jung's use of Eckhart in these passages sheds considerable light on the deeper religious implications of Jung's psychology and also illuminates Eckhart's experience through Jung's appropriation of it. Volume six is Jung's first work after his painful break with Freud. In this volume, Jung looks for models of religious experience that would help him come to terms with his frightening experience of the psyche in the wake of the break with Freud and which would be helpful in the formulation of his own still developing understanding of the psyche.

The first major feature of this newer understanding of the role of the psyche in the generation of religious experience which Jung relates to his appreciation of Eckhart is what he calls the relativity of God. With this phrase Jung means that God and human consciousness are so intimately linked that they are functions of each other. This intimacy supposes a mutual dependence and a mutual inter-action which might accurately be described by both Eckhart and Jung as a process of mutual redemption. Thus the idea of a God who is wholly other than humanity and ontologically discontinuous from human consciousness is denied in principle by Jung in this early work and throughout the remainder of his corpus. This he makes explicit when he writes:

> The "relativity of God," as I understand it, denotes a point of view that does not conceive of God as "absolute," i.e., wholly "cut off" from man and existing outside and beyond all human

conditions, but as in a certain sense dependent on him; it also implies a reciprocal and essential relation between man and God, whereby man can be understood as a function of God and God as a psychological function of man.[21]

Later in this passage Jung implies that the God who is understood as a metaphysical absolute and not as a "function of the unconscious" betrays "...a complete unawareness of the fact that God's action springs from one's own inner being."[22] In these passages Jung makes it clear that an approach to the phenomenon of religion, from the viewpoint of theology or of any discipline, which would remain unaware of the intra-psychic origins of religion universally, would be victimized by an unconsciousness which would mislocate beyond the psyche the generative origins of a reality which is its product. Moreover, in these passages Jung makes equally clear that he considers Eckhart to have been among the first to realize that the human experience of God originates wholly from within the psyche, though obviously from a source within the psyche transcendent to the ego.

Jung then goes on to elaborate the implications of this insight in terms of the psychological consequences of the withdrawal of the projection of God and its psychic internalization. The operative passage that Jung uses from Eckhart in this discussion reads, "The soul is not blissful because she is in God, she is blissful because God is in her."[23] He then goes on to show how the soul loses its bliss when it is in God and how it recovers its bliss when God is in it. In doing this Jung describes two distinct modes in which the soul can be in God and so forgo its bliss.

In the first instance the soul projects the energies that give rise to the sense of God onto some external object or person. This is the primitive psychology of tondi or manna in which the divine energy that belongs to oneself is projected onto someone or something else in the creation of an external divinity or representative of divinity. The recovery of this projection is therefore also a recovery of the energy that had been given away in the creation of the divine reality beyond oneself with which the soul had

---

21.   C. G. Jung, *Psychological Types*, CW 6, par. 412, p. 243.

22.   *Ibid.*, CW 6, par. 413, p. 243.

23.   *Ibid.*, CW 6, par. 418, p. 246.

identified. In this sense the introjection of the projection places God back in the soul with the bliss attendant to the self-possession and assurance which characterizes a consciousness living out of its internal divine energies now in its service.[24]

But the second sense of the soul moving from a state of a blissless being in God to the bliss of God being in it is far more complex, because it describes a wholly internal process in which the soul moving into the well spring of all life within the psyche stands in danger of being overwhelmed by what Jung calls its creative *dynamis*,[25] later identified with the basis in the psyche for the experience of God.[26] This he describes as a power in which the soul could be drowned in the creative potential of the deeper unconscious were it not able to establish its own autonomy and mediate the creativity of the depths of the psyche to the ego. Jung writes of the hazards of this psychic situation and its ideal resolution in Eckhart's terms in these words:

> When, says Eckhart, the soul is in God it is not "blissful," for when this organ of perception is overwhelmed by the divine *dynamis* it is by no means a happy state. But when God is in the soul, i.e., when the soul becomes the vessel for the unconscious and makes itself an image or symbol of it, this is a truly happy state.[27]

What Jung is here describing, using Eckhart's religious imagery, becomes the ground movement of psychic energies in his own psychological paradigm later described in this passage as the diastolic and systolic movement of psychic energies, terms borrowed from the medical description of blood moving into and out of the heart. As appropriated by Jung, this circularity means that the soul must enter into, or allow to enter into it, the deeper and divine energies of the unconscious, which it in turn mediates to consciousness. Ideally, in this circular movement the soul mediates to consciousness the energies she herself derives from the deeper unconscious

---

24.   *Ibid.*, CW 6, par. 421, p. 247.

25.   *Ibid.*, CW 6, par. 425, pp. 250, 251.

26.   *Ibid.*, CW 6, par. 430, p. 255.

27.   *Ibid.*, CW 6, par. 425, p. 251.

in a hopefully ongoing and ever surer rhythm. Could the soul not enter or mediate these energies to the ego, the ego would be sterilized by its barren imprisonment in the world of consciousness. Were the soul to drown in them, the ego would drown with her in what Jung calls "the immersion in the flood and source."[28]

In fact, this "immersion" is precisely the reality Eckhart refers to as the "breakthrough," which implies a total lack of differentiation between the soul and God so that no other relation than unqualified unity is possible. Though the fear of permanent loss in this *dynamis* and its psychotic consequences are real for Jung, they seem never to have troubled Eckhart. Rather, Eckhart's ability to enter into this kind of self-loss in God apparently remained as available to him as did his confidence that he could return from it. What Jung does for modernity is to show to it and to its understanding of the psyche that such depth exists and must, in one form or another, be accessible in the processes of psychological development. Thus the perils of establishing a healthy commerce with the deeper levels of the unconscious belongs to all of psychic life in its experience of maturation which, in this sense and at this level, is always religious in nature, whether the idiom of its expression be religious or not. Jung is here simply using Eckhart's religious experience and expression as a dramatic instance of what is at stake in these delicate and inescapable negotiations in every life.

From this point Jung moves quickly to the dialectic at the heart of his and Eckhart's thought. The soul which is in some sense the creature of God is also needed by God to mediate God's energies to consciousness. In this role she is the mother of God as the vehicle through which God becomes conscious in human consciousness. This reciprocity between the soul and the unconscious is the universal psychological foundation which Jung gives to the specific and central theme of God's birth in the soul in Eckhart's thought. It would also provide the psychological basis for the assertion by Eckhart and other mystics that God seeks to be born again and again in the soul. This divine lust is an expression of the divine need to become fully conscious in human consciousness through the mediating function of the soul in such a

---

28.   *Ibid.*, CW 6, par. 430, p. 255.

way as to complete divinity in the completion of human consciousness. Jung sums up this aspect of his reflection on Eckhart and the mutual dependency of God and the human in the latter's theology and spirituality in these terms, "Here Eckhart states bluntly that God is dependent on the soul, and at the same time, that the soul is the birthplace of God."[29]

It is not surprising, then, that Jung, in his most extensive treatment of Gnosticism in volume nine ii of the *Collected Works*, associates Eckhart's experience with it. He does so because of the gnostic experience of a unity of opposites which precedes all differentiation and yet in which all differentiation is latent. This is the famous pleroma of Jung's *Septem Sermones ad Mortuos*.[30] This dimension of the psyche Jung relates to Eckhart's understanding of the Godhead and to that experience of the Godhead which Eckhart calls the breakthrough, an experience in which all differentiation in God and between God and creature is dissolved.[31] Jung writes accurately, though with that same sense of paradox characteristic of Eckhart himself, that such an experience would cause unconsciousness in anyone who would undergo it since all consciousness is related to differentiation. In a line Eckhart himself would enjoy, Jung states, "As the Godhead is essentially unconscious, so too is the man who lives in God."[32] Indeed, Eckhart's understanding of true poverty and humility demands an immersion and self-loss in this dimension of being. For Eckhart the most impoverishing act of humility is the achievement of that state of reality wherein the individual and deity become one beyond difference. But one must then return from such unity, and as one does, the reality of God is born again in the soul and empowers the individual for the challenge of life. With Jung the repetitive and circular movement of the ego into this pleroma and back to its engagement in conscious life is the base meaning of incarnation and the base movement of what he calls individuation.

---

29. *Ibid.*, CW 6, par. 426, p. 251.

30. C. G. Jung, *Memories, Dreams, Reflections, op. cit.*, p. 378f.

31. C. G. Jung, CW 9ii, par. 301, p. 193.

32. *Ibid.*

The same themes are operative in Jung's linking Eckhart with the sartori experience of the Zen tradition in volume eleven of the *Collected Works*.[33] Here Jung deals with the link between Eckhart and Zen as two forms of spirituality sharply contrasting with spiritualities which offer access to the unconscious either through a set of images other than one's own, as is the case in the Ignatian exercises, or through ecclesial mediation based on the eliciting of expected responses, as would be the case, for instance, in Protestant, or for that matter, any formal religious service or liturgy.[34] What Jung is directing attention to here is the possibility of an immediate access to that layer of one's psyche which precedes images and from which all images flow into consciousness. Again the implication is that the deeper one moves into one's interiority, the closer does one approach the imageless ground of all imagery. Later in this section Jung identifies this ground with what he calls the "matrix mind," and describes it as the source not only of all imagery but of all the meaningful forms of expressions and disciplines of which the conscious mind is capable.[35]

Before leaving Jung's treatment of Eckhart, a moment should be devoted to Jung's attachment to Eckhartian material which is certainly apocryphal or spurious, but, according to Josef Quint, the editor of the modern edition of Jung's German works, faithful to Eckhart's spirit.[36] One such story has to do with the appearance of the little naked boy to Eckhart. Jung cites the story four times through his *Collected Works*.[37] As recorded in Evans, the tale tells of a verbal exchange between Eckhart and the child. In response to Eckhart's questions the child replies that he came from God who

33.   C. G. Jung, "Foreward to Suzuki's 'Introduction to Zen Buddhism,'" CW 11, par. 887, p. 543f.

34.   *Ibid.*, CW 11, par. 893, pp. 547, 548.

35.   *Ibid.*, CW 11, par. 899, p. 552.

36.   Josef Quint, Introduction, *Die deutschen und lateinischen Werke* (Stuttgart, 1938), p. xiii, as cited and translated in James M. Clark and John V. Skinner, Preface, *Treatises and Sermons of Meister Eckhart* (New York: Harper & Bros., 1958), pp. 24-25.

37.   C. G. Jung, "The Archetypes of the Collective Unconscious," CW 9i, par. 268, p. 158 and *ibid.*, "The Phenomenology of Spirit in Fairy Tales," par. 396, p. 215, fn, 8; "Foreword to Suzuki's 'Introduction to Zen Buddhism,'" CW 11, par. 882, p. 541; *Mysterium Coniunctionis*, CW 14, par. 379, p. 282.

dwells in virtuous hearts, that he will return to God by leaving all creatures, and that he is a king whose kingdom is in his (the child's) own heart. Obviously impressed, Eckhart takes the child to his cell and offers him the coat of his choice. The child refuses any gift. To take one would mean that he would no longer be king. The legend ends, "It was God himself that he had with him a little spell."[38]

Jung interprets the boy as a symbol of the divine child at work in Eckhart's psyche and in volume 9i relates the child not only to the future but to the past as providing that rootedness in the past - and by implication in eternity - that enables one to move into the future without debilitating self-loss, especially in times of stressful change.[39] Given Eckhart's difficult historical role of ushering in a fragile consciousness destined to shape the future but deemed heretical by his peers in his own time, one can appreciate the grounding and stabilizing image of the divine child, the self, which enabled him to bear the weight of the future out of what he felt to be fidelity both to the depth of his own experience and to his Christian past.

Jung was also fascinated by the apocryphal tale of Eckhart's daughter, who appeared one day and defined herself negatively as not imbued with any feminine or masculine role but, because identified with none, possessed of all. "I am not either virgin or spouse, not man nor wife nor widow nor lady nor lord nor wench nor thrall."[40] Jung, as did Eckhart before him, marvels at such a woman as an image of Eckhart's anima. But he could as well have seen in her a powerful and many-faced wisdom figure not unlike the Gnostic Sophia.

A final apocryphal figure in the Eckhart corpus to whom Jung never refers but whom he surely would have appreciated is the figure of Sister Katerina.[41] Many versions of this legend remain extant. It describes a

---

38. Evans, *op. cit.*, vol. 1, p. 488.

39. C. G. Jung, "The Psychology of the Child Archetype," CW 9i, pars. 267, 268, pp. 157, 158.

40. C. G. Jung, *Mysterium Coniunctionis*, CW 14, par. 102, pp. 87, 88. Jung is citing from Evans, *op. cit.*, pp. 438, 439.

41. "Appendix, The Sister Catherine Treatise," Elvira Borgstadt, *Meister Eckhart* (New York: Paulist Press, 1986), pp. 349-387.

process which begins with a woman penitent coming to a confessor for spiritual guidance. Much of the initial guidance is very traditional asceticism. But gradually the penitent is weaned from the confessor and comes more directly under the unmediated influence of the Holy Ghost. After a period "in exile" from her confessor, she returns as someone he does not recognize and makes a confession that reveals her own advanced spiritual state to him. As her progress continues, she reaches a state in which she can say without qualification, "Sir, rejoice with me I am God."[42] But this initial experience is preliminary to its confirmation in a subsequent experience, a three-day trance.[43] After this experience, not only is she now God but permanently so. Her experientially based conviction is that she can never lose her native divinity. The treatise, though not Eckhart's, is in many ways so representative of his mind that it cannot but raise the question of the orthodoxy of the fuller implications of his experience and its expression.[44]

An interesting twist in the interaction between the confessor and the woman is that her spiritual progress outstrips his, and in the end she becomes his advisor, and indeed, tells him in the conclusion of the story that he is in no condition yet to follow her into the depths of the Godhead from which she has returned and to which she is united without fear of loss, indeed, without the possibility of loss. Internalized, the story would capture the movement of the soul into the unconscious and her return to consciousness with an experience of the imperishable point at which her humanity and divinity coincide, something that only those who undergo the experience can comprehend. Thus Eckhart's daughter might well be his anima, and as such the mediator to him of his pervasive sense of the birth of the son of God in his soul, which ultimately connects him with the Godhead, the ground of his being. In this manner she would mediate that unity between the human and

---

42. Evans, *op. cit.*, vol. 1, p. 325; Borgstadt, *op. cit.*, p. 358, where the translation is "...I have become God."

43. Evans, *ibid.* Here the statement is "I am confirmed." Borgstadt translates, "I am granted everlasting bliss."

44. For a discussion of this issue and the relevant commentators, *cf.* B. McGinn, "Introduction" *Meister Eckhart* (New York: Paulist Press, 1986), pp. 10-14.

divine which allows no distinction and forces whoever experiences it to say with Sister Catherine, "Sir, rejoice with me I am God."

Let us turn now to a summary of the distinctive features of Eckhart's thought and the reason for its rejection by orthodoxy, then and now, before a final summation of the psycho-spiritual consequences of the discussion. In dealing with the theological imagination, medieval or modern, two options are possible. One can begin with God and trace the emmanation of humanity from its divine source, or one can begin with humanity and trace the way back to its origin. Let us begin our treatment of Eckhart with the first option, how he envisages the line from God to humanity, with a necessarily brief and systematic treatment of Eckhart's position on it.

Eckhart distinguished himself from theologians before and after his work by unmistakably positing a quaternity in the divine life itself. He does this by clearly distinguishing between the Godhead and its derivative, God as trinitarian. A contemporary leading Eckhart scholar, Reiner Schurmann, makes this point explicitly and comments extensively on it when he cites Eckhart's dramatic formulation "God and Godhead are as distinct as heaven and earth."[45] The Godhead which precedes and gives rise to the Trinitarian God is totally without differentiation, yet is somehow that from which all differentiation proceeds, including that of the Trinity. John Caputo agrees with Schurmann and formulates Eckhart's experience of the quaternity in God in these terms: "The Godhead is the absolute unity, the negation of all multiplicity, not only of the multiplicity of creatures but even of the multiplicity of Persons in the divine Trinity."[46]

Whatever personal experience led him to it, and his works are void of any biographical indicators in this matter, Eckhart has, in the distinction between Godhead and Trinity, recovered in the historical context of fourteenth-century Christianity the deepest meaning of the great Goddess or

---

45.   Reiner Schurmann, *Meister Eckhart* (Bloomington: Indiana University Press, 1978), p. 114. The citation is from the sermon *Nolite timere eos* in Franz Pfeifer, *Deutsche Mystiker des viersehnten Jarhunderts*, vol. 2, *Meister Eckhart, Predigten und Traktate* (Leipzig, 1857, and Aalen, 1962), p. 18. In the Evans translation, *Meister Eckhart*, by Franz Pfeifer, (London: John M. Watkins, 1947) it is sermon 56 and the citation appears in vol. 1, p. 142. On the distinction between Godhead and Trinity, *cf.* Schurmann, pp. 45, 46, 114.

46.   J. Caputo, *op. cit.*, p. 106.

great Mother, who in his paradigm must be understood to give birth to or mother the Trinity itself. One tragic limitation of Christian symbolism is that the closest it can get to this aspect of Eckhart's experience is in its imagination of the furthest and most generative dimension of the Trinity, which it names "Father." What it needs in this respect is a recovery of the experience and symbolic expression of the Mother power which precedes the consequent differentiation and activity within deity. The symbol of the Trinity adequately depicts this secondary or penultimate dimension of deity. But it is largely incapable of mediating the precedent power of the Great Mother and so contributes to a patriarchal and truncated consciousness by functioning to remove those living under the symbol from a full or heightened experience of her power. Though this discussion may seem remote from current cultural concerns and reality, much is at stake in terms of individual health and social survival. For Eckhart in the fourteenth century and for Jung in the twentieth, it is precisely in cyclical reimmersion in her renewing nothingness that both locate humanity's most profound union with God, from which it derives its energies to renew itself in configurations of expanded sensitivity and more universal embrace. Needless to say, this renewal would also dissolve currently divisive and potentially terminal faiths, in religious or political form, toward a survival consciousness beyond our current spiritual congealment in mutually inimical "faith" communities.

Eckhart describes this great creative ocean out of which the Trinity evolves as in no way moved by its own dynamic to express itself beyond itself. Eckhart is cited as saying, "The essence of the Godhead begets not."[47] It rests wholly content within its own immensity, the ultimate resource for "letting be" or "living without why." Thus the movement back to unity with this dimension of God or the psyche brings with it that detached consciousness, by no means without a capacity for consequent engagement, that is so essential an aspect of Eckhart's experience and spirituality. Generally speaking, this aspect of his thought is what Eckhart calls *gelazenheit*, which can be translated with a more traditional spiritual term

---

47.   Evans, *op. cit.*, vol. 1, Sermon 58, *Divine Understanding*, p. 148. This sermon may not be authentic, but this citation is true to Eckhart's mind.

such as "resignation" or "detachment" but often finds translation in a more popular modern idiom as "letting be" or, in a phrase that resonates with Heidegger, "releasement."[48] One of Eckhart's favourite ways of describing this consciousness was in the ability "to live without why."[49] For Eckhart the ability to thus live was obviously a residue of his experience of total dissolution in that dimension of God he called the Godhead, where such living without why characterizes the cosmic ground of all that differentiates from it.

His treatment of this resting passivity in the furthest reach of deity, the Godhead, appears to be the basis of some tension in his thought, because obviously she did break her resting within herself, first giving birth to the Trinity and through the Trinity to what is called creation. Otherwise Eckhart could not have pointed to her reality in the fourteenth century nor Jung to Eckhart's pointing to her reality in the twentieth. Had she not broken her containment, paradoxically without why in doing so, nothing would be.

The way that Eckhart imagines reality, including the Trinity, to emerge from its maternal precedent is of great interest and is given initial attention in his condemnation. For he thinks that, once that process described as the Father's generating the Son and uniting with the Son in the Spirit begins, - as a removal from its maternal precedent - the process, of its own nature, necessarily flows into creation. Thus, in the fourteenth century Eckhart strikes those notes destined to re-emerge in the nineteenth century which would see history as a necessary expression of divinity in which alone divinity could find its realization and completion. In theological language this would mean that creation and human consciousness become a necessary and organic continuation of the emergence of the trinity from the Goddess and that in created historical consciousness the process moves to its completion. As the Trinity emmanates from the Mother Goddess, so does creation from the Trinity in a single process that culminates in human consciousness. It is in this context that Eckhart terms the life of the Trinity a

---

48. This term is used extensively in Schurmann's work.

49. Schurmann adds to the ways of describing this state the term "dehiscence," *op. cit.*, pp. 111-121.

bullitio, an image of a boiling or seething vitality, which culminates in a necessary *ebullitio*, a boiling over into the reality of creation.[50]

In thus conceiving of the Trinity's emmanation from its precedent and creation's emmanation from the Trinity, Eckhart denies the validity of any imaginal situation in which a self-sufficient God existed in magnificent isolation from eternity. As his condemnation makes clear, he argues that God creates as soon as God exists out of the need for humanity to complete the divine life in humanity. The first two articles of his condemnation, which the condemnation alleges Eckhart admitted were reflective of his preaching,[51] provide him with a precision on these points his own formulations often lacked, a strange and self-defeating contribution by the Inquisition effectively contributing to the posterity of his mind. These condemned articles read:

> The first article. When someone once asked him why God had not created the world earlier, he answered then, as he does now, that God could not have created the world earlier, because a thing cannot act before it exists, and so as soon as God existed he created the world.
> The third article. Also, in the one and the same time when God was, when he begot his co-eternal Son as God equal to himself in all things, he also created the world.[52]

Again, the further implications of a divine necessity to create motivated by a divine need to become conscious in human consciousness, insights culminating in Hegel's philosophy in the nineteenth century and in Jung's psychology in the twentieth, are clearly present in the thirteenth condemned article:

> The thirteenth article. Whatever is proper to the divine nature, all that is proper to the just and divine man. Because of that, this man performs whatever God performs, and he created heaven and earth together with God, and he is the

---

50. For a brief theological description of this process, *cf.* Bernard McGinn, Theological Summary, *Meister Eckhart* (New York: Paulist Press, 1981), p. 31.

51. *Cf.* E. Colledge, Historical Data, *Meister Eckhart*, *op. cit.*, p. 12.

52. "In agro dominico," (March 27, 1329), articles one and three, in *Meister Eckhart*, *op. cit.*, pp. 77, 78.

90

begetter of the Eternal Word, and God would not know how to
do anything without such a man.[53]

In thus making human consciousness a creator of the world with God
and the locus of divine redemption in an ontological sense, Eckhart goes far
beyond similar sounding, more traditional statements about humanity as co-
creator with God. The vigorous pantheism at the core of his thought reduces
these formulations, based as they are on a self-sufficient transcendent God,
to the level of pious sentimentality. Through clearly stating that the
emmanation of the Word from the Father necessarily continues in the form
of the divine compulsion to create and be born into human consciousness
where the process completes itself, Eckhart established an organic link
between divinity and humanity too intimate for orthodoxy, certainly then and
probably now, as witnessed in the recent condemnation of Mathew Fox, O.P.,
for his efforts to revive these themes in what Fox calls a creation-centred
spirituality.[54]

This radical dimension of Eckhart's thought is evident in one of his
more striking formulations, which captures much of his mind and the
experience behind it. He says that in the one Word two things are spoken or
that he hears two things.[55] By this formulation Eckhart means that God's
expression in trinitarian life cannot be separated from God's expression in
creation, since they are two aspects of one process. He thus founds his
pantheism on both humanity's experience of its continuity with Trinitarian
life and with the Word of God in that life and on the divine need to become
real in the created expression of that Word. The nineteenth century defined
this latter position, I think rightly, as panlogism.

It is in this aspect of his vision, the divine necessity to become fully
conscious in creation, that Eckhart introduces a second quaternity in his
thought. Just as the reality of deity has a fourth dimension, (the first
quaternity) in the Godhead or Goddess preceding and birthing the Trinity, so
also does the Trinity have to express itself in human consciousness as the

53. "In agrico dominico," *op. cit.*, p. 79.

54. *Cf.* for example, M. Fox, *Breakthrough: Meister Eckhart's Creation Spirituality in New Translation*, Introduction and Commentaries by M. Fox (Garden City: Image Books, 1980).

55. "Selections from the Commentary on John," Meister Eckhart, *op. cit.*, p. 148.

fourth and as its completion. Thus, in his theology of creation Eckhart takes a position functionally identical with Jung's in insisting that trinitarian models must currently cede to quaternitarian models in the interest of humanity's wholeness.[56] This means with both Eckhart and Jung that religious paradigms of a self-sufficient deity even potentially discontinuous from creation and human consciousness must be reversed in the interests of the now dawning experience that only in human consciousness does deity itself become conscious and conscious of its totality so that neither creator nor creature can any longer evade joint responsibility for anything that is. From the human perspective, this means that humanity can no longer avoid its basic moral task in history, that of serving as the vehicle of God's becoming fully conscious and fully human. As Jung makes clear in his "Answer to Job," since this process involves the full surfacing of the divine self-contradiction with its volatility and destructive capacity, the human adventure may now be entering into a new phase of psycho-spirituality in which it will be called upon consciously to enter its psychic interiority in the process of its survival and enhancement. It marks the end of the age of projection and raises the question of whether or not any existing religious tradition living under a projectionist understanding of its myth in the service of any of the numerous one and only transcendent Gods can aid humanity in its current need to free itself from such potentially terminal consciousness.

Eckhart goes on to challenge the Christian imagination, both medieval and modern, when he refuses to isolate the Christ figure as an individual or the meaning of Christianity as hanging on individual historical events. He does this by asking what good it does him if Christ is born historically in Mary and not in himself. A typical formulation would read, "St. Augustine says this birth is always happening. But if it happen not in me what does it profit me?"[57] And when the Word is born in his soul, Eckhart affirms and was condemned for affirming that the individual then is another Christ, *is* that Christic reality in which the individual then participates.

---

56.   The *locus classicus* where Jung makes this paradigm shift is in "A Psychological Approach to the Dogma of the Trinity," CW 11, sec. 5, "The Problem of the Fourth," p. 164f. His "Answer to Job," *ibid.*, p. 357f is a late poetic-systematic working out of its implications.

57.   Evans. vol. 1, *op. cit*, p. 3.

92

Therefore, articles ten to twelve in his condemnation condemn the unqualified identity Eckhart establishes between the Christian and Christ. A selection from the tenth article captures Eckhart's radical mind on this matter. It reads, "In the same way, when the sacrament bread is changed into Christ's Body, I am so changed into him that he makes me his one existence, and not just similar."[58]

This position is identical with Jung's spirituality, which would refuse to locate the true imitation of Christ in an external adherence to events of the past, often of a miraculous nature so grotesque in their uniqueness as to make them freakish to modern sensitivities. Rather, Jung, like Eckhart, would understand this imitation in a true re-experiencing of the archetypal truth of the Christ event. Thus Eckhart's insistence that the birth of God in the soul identifies that soul with the Word of God and so with the experienced reality of Christ anticipates Jung's psychological formulation of the same experience six hundred years later as that of the birth of the self in consciousness.

Eckhart's treatment of the birth of God in the soul serves as the point to switch perspectives from the flow of creation from God to the tracing of his experience of the soul's return to God. Moderns now see this return centred on two distinct movements in one process, the birth of the Word in the soul and the breakthrough. Eckhart understands the process of voluntary poverty and humility as one which strips the individual of all that could prevent the soul from being that virgin in whom the Word is conceived and through whom the soul becomes God.[59] The ultimate act of humility for Eckhart is the recovery of one's natural divinity. My own tracking of this process leads me to agree with modern commentators like Caputo and Schurmann that what Eckhart means by the birth of God in the soul is a discrete stage preliminary to an even deeper co-inhesion of humanity and divinity. Rather than lead the individual in whom the birth of God happens back to the life of conscious engagement immediately, the event serves as the

---

58. "In Agro dominico," *op. cit.*, article ten, p. 78.

59. This point central to all of Eckhart's thought is well developed in his sermon, "Blessed Are The Poor." *Cf.* Schurmann's translation and commentary, *op. cit.*, pp. 214-220.

occasion for yet a deeper ingression into the divine reality, Eckhart's breakthrough. This process involves the mutual loss of all identity and differentiation on the part of both Trinity and humanity in a total mutual obliteration and so self-loss of one in the other. If God is nothing and the individual is nothing, can they be anything but one? Thus for Eckhart the furthest reach of unity with the Godhead takes place in a total dissolution in the cosmic Mother or Goddess. In his imagery - which has to be self-contradictory to capture this re-entry into the nothingness which mothers all - one recovers one's eternal and ineradicable truth, one's unqualified unity with deity in a place where even God, as differentiated and so as other than the individual, cannot enter. In this state Eckhart identifies himself without qualification with the unmoved mover, in medieval terms, with God as the source of the totality. This is how Eckhart describes the experience:

> For in this breakthrough it is bestowed upon me that I and God are one. There I am what I was and I neither diminish nor grow, for there I am an immovable cause that moves all things. Now God no longer finds a place in man, for man gains with this poverty what he has been eternally and evermore will remain.[60]

The unity with God beyond differentiation which Eckhart strives to describe in this typical passage in no way implies a permanent disengagement from the world of the multiple. On the contrary, it is from this apparently total removal from conscious life that one then derives the energy to re-engage it. In a reversal of the usual meaning of the Martha - Mary biblical story, Eckhart reads Martha as someone whose renewal in the nothingness from which all proceeds has freed her to serve, while Mary, who has yet to experience and be transformed by these depths, must sit at the knee of the Christ figure and await the enabling experience which Martha has undergone as the basis of her total activity in the world.[61]

Let us conclude with a final comparison, beginning with points of agreement between the two men. The basic shift of perspective in the religious paradigm of each man is that God and humanity are so intimately

60.   Meister Eckhart, "Blessed Are the Poor," Schurmann's translation, *op. cit.*, p. 219.
61.   Meister Eckhart, sermon, "Mary and Martha," Evans, *op. cit.*, vol. 2, p. 90f.

connected that they are functions of each other. This common feature of their experience explains the profoundly pantheistic element that enlivens the thought and spirit of each and gives to each the assurance that the sense of God in whatever form it might take is a universal and ineradicable human capacity.

But theirs is no simple pantheism, for in the commerce between the divine and human poles of the single cosmic organism, a process of mutual redemption is in progress. On this point both would agree that God was compelled to create humanity in order to become fully conscious in it. To this basic agreement Jung would add the note that a major feature in the divine compulsion is God's necessity to constellate and resolve in human consciousness the contradictions divinity could neither perceive nor resolve in its own life. This I take to be the substance of Jung's late work on Job.

More than this, both Eckhart and Jung describe the dynamics involved in the mutual redemption of humanity and divinity in a discernibly similar manner. For both, a consciousness, aware of its alienated otherness from its source, re-enters that source in its own depths. In this inner journey the pilgrim consciousness moves behind the opposites which are latent in that source, symbolized by the Trinity, there to recover a consciousness vested with an enhanced vitality for life and a peculiar capacity for the unification of its contradictions at the conscious level personally and socially. This capacity is itself made possible by its experience of the one source of all life which it brings back to consciousness on its return. This accounts for the powers of reconciliation that frequently attach to mystical consciousness as it impacts on surrounding society and for the central role such power for reconciliation plays in the theology of Eckhart and the psychology of Jung.

However, the unmediated nature of this access to the further reaches of humanity where it intersects without hindrance with deity can be troublesome to orthodoxy, as it obviously was with Eckhart and to some lesser extent with Jung. The reason is that orthodoxy, as the provider of the religious ideology on which the religious status quo is grounded, is often vested with a lesser vision and with a vested interest in its maintenance. Speaking of the satori experience which he relates to Eckhart's, Jung writes:

> There is nothing in our civilization to foster these strivings, not even the Church, the custodian of religious values. Indeed, it is the function of the Church to oppose all original experience, because this can only be unorthodox.[62]

Thus, in Jung's opinion, the ecclesial rejection of Eckhart's experience remains into our century a dark, self-contradictory necessity for the survival of the Church as institution.

Jung has contributed immensely to the modern appropriation and appreciation of Eckhart by showing his experience to be grounded in an experience of the deepest level of the psyche, whose surfacing in the natural maturation of the psyche is always for Jung intensely religious. This is evident in Jung's appreciation of the master symbols of the self. The mandala, the *anthropos*, the alchemical *unus mundus*, and synchronicity all evidence a consciousness moving toward a unity within oneself and with the totality beyond oneself out of one's experienced groundedness in the source of the totality as one's personal ground. Thus Jung provides the modern with a critical and more conscious capacity to respond to and appreciate Eckhart's experience, indeed even to assimilate it personally.

In doing this Jung brings a hermeneutic to bear on Eckhart's experience, illuminating it in ways that Eckhart himself could hardly be expected to understand in his own time. Jung's contention that Eckhart's experience is natural to the human psyche and, in one form or another, implicated in psychic maturation universally implies no loss of the sense of the sacredness of the experience. On the contrary, Jung's appreciation and appropriation of Eckhart is far from a form of psychological reductionism. Rather, it shows to our times the enduring value of Eckhart's religious experience as proceeding from the deepest strata of our common human nature and holds out to contemporary consciousness the possibility of a universal, sympathetic, human relatedness based on a profound sense of the inhesion of each individual and existent in their sacred common origin.

But to do this Jung, like Eckhart, had to move from a trinitarian to a quaternitarian paradigm and introduce a conception of humanity's relation to

---

62.   C. G. Jung, "Foreward to Suzuki's 'Introduction to Zen Buddhism,'" CW 11, par. 903, p. 553.

God which is abrasive to at least Western orthodoxy. The newer paradigm would demand radical recasting of such central themes as the gratuity of creation and the nature of the fall, since both Eckhart and Jung imply that the universal truth of original sin is the sin of becoming conscious. Moreover, the gratuity of God in the gracing of humanity is radically compromised, in the new paradigm, by a divine self-interest which undermines the traditional assertion that divinity could be unaffected by the outcome of the human adventure. The new paradigm of the commerce between divinity and humanity in their mutual gracing would have to entrust to humanity's response to the divine need to become conscious in it a far greater importance and initiative than traditional Christian theologies of grace can possibly provide.

For these reasons contemporary Jungian scholars such as Murray Stein, while clearly perceiving the above implications of the shift to a quaternitarian paradigm, perceive equally clearly that it cannot be mediated or encouraged by ecclesial communities grounded on the Christian myth with its trinitarian and self-sufficient deity. Stein captures the full and radical import of the implications of Jung's psychology, which we have amplified through Eckhart as one of its most significant historical precedents, when he writes:

> And to my mind, it is highly dubious that traditional Christianity ever will, or could if it wanted to, voluntarily die and be reborn into the next phase of evolution as envisioned by Jung.[63]

Stein goes on to express little hope that the transformation of religious consciousness demanded by the fuller implications of Jung's psychology can be brought to society through "the tradition's leadership."[64] There is much to be said for Stein's intimation that the theological implications of Jung's psychology and psycho-spirituality, though already brought to some consciousness in the West six hundred years ago in

---

63.   Murray Stein, *Jung's Treatment of Christianity: The Psychotherapy of a Religious Tradition* (Wilmette, Illinois: Chiron Publications, 1985), all of ch. 5, but especially pp. 185, 186.

64.   *Ibid.*, p. 188.

Eckhart's thought, continue to appear as unacceptable to today's Inquisitors as they did to their fourteenth-century predecessors.

Before concluding, it should be pointed out, as promised, that, though Jung was helped by Eckhart in the formation of his own understanding of the psyche, there are elements in Eckhart's work that might serve reciprocally to deepen Jung's. A familiarity with Eckhart's primary work seems to point to an experience of so complete a divestiture of individuality in the entrance into those dimensions of human interiority where humanity and divinity merge without difference, that a Jungian interpretation of the experience forces one to wonder if he did not plumb a depth from which even Jung stepped back. One must ask if Eckhart went deeper into the psyche than its archetypal base where Jung, at least in his writings, felt he had struck bottom. Jung, even in his conception of the collective unconscious, locates there the latent power of the archetypes which, though only potential, do contain some definition, some differentiation, however "contaminated" they are with each other due to the lack of any differentiating consciousness. But one cannot avoid the feeling that Eckhart experienced some void beyond even the archetypal world in that experience he calls the breakthrough.

Obviously Jung could appreciate and was manifestly aware of this dimension of the psyche in his linking Eckhart with Zen, and again in his break work with Freud, where the unconscious as oceanic comes to the fore as it was later to be depicted in some of Jung's alchemical imagery. But the experience of so radical a self-loss is not formally a component of the model of the psyche and its working which Jung left us. The question might be asked if this could be due to the terror that attached to Jung's first experience of the deeper unconscious and its powers in the painful period following his break with Freud.[65] Jung's inaugural experience may have left him with a residual fear or even terror, and certainly with an abiding respect, for the consuming or devouring powers of that infinite abyss beneath every centre of consciousness, where Eckhart apparently felt so much at home and to which he had apparently such easy access. Since time has closed over the possibility

---

65.   *Cf.* C. G. Jung, *Memories, Dreams, Reflections, op. cit.*, ch. VI, Confrontation with the Unconscious.

98

of recovering the personal experience that lies behind the heritage Eckhart left us, much of this line of inquiry must remain speculation. But Jung himself would thunder that such speculation was far from idle and to be neglected at our peril when he writes:

> These considerations have made me extremely cautious in my approach to the further metaphysical significance that may possibly underlie archetypal statements. There is nothing to stop their ramifications from penetrating to the very ground of the universe. We alone are the dumb ones if we fail to notice it.[66]

The reason Jung felt that it would be dumb to refuse to pursue to the very ground of the universe the implications of archetypal experience is one shared by Eckhart. For both men the depth of the penetration of human interiority by individual and society is directly proportionate to the healing and integrating wealth brought back to individual and social life from such excursions into the healing depths. For Jung and Eckhart, what was brought back was a renewal of the zest for a life balanced in itself and moving to an extended and unqualified embrace of humanity in all its expressions. Such an extended embrace was made possible through contact with the one source of the teeming human multiplicity dwelling in the depth of every single human being and longing to become conscious in every human life. Out of the intensity of this experience in his own life, Jung, and hopefully greater constituencies in the modern world, would gladly join in Eckhart's most paradoxial prayer, "I pray to God to rid me of God."[67] For both Jung and Eckhart were confident that when lesser and divisive Gods and faiths are lost, the loser is freer, the rest of us safer, and the community richer in every way.

---

66.   CW 11, par. 295, p. 200.

67.   From "Blessed are the Poor," *Meister Eckhart*, ed. Reiner Schurmann (Bloomington: Indiana University Press, 1978), pp. 219.

Index

A

"A priori" source of consciousness, 43
Africa, Jung's experiences in, 42
Albert the Great, 74
Alchemical work, of Jung, 46, 74
Allah, 50
Androgyny, Jungian concept of, 56-57
Animal life, Jungian concept of human continuity with, 42-43
Animus, 57-59
Anselm, 18
"Answer to Job" (Jung), 91
Anthropos, 37, 95
Aquinas, Thomas, 5-6, 74
Archetypes,
    archetypal experience, 58
    in collective unconscious, 15
The Assumption, 53
Atheism, Tillich on, 10
Aurum non vulgas, 46

B

Baader, Franz, 76
Biblical imagination,
    Jung's critique of, 1-39
Boehme, Jacob, 71
Bonaventure, 36

C

Caputo, John, 86
Catherine, Sister, 86
Catholicism,
    Marian doctrine, 52
    theology, 13-14
Catholicism.,
    see also Christianity
Chardin, Teilhard de, 13-14, 64
Christ figure, 3, 65, 91
Christian imagination, 14, 91
Christian myth, violence and, 16-17
Christianity, Jung on, 1-39

Collected Works (Jung), 47-48, 70-71, 73, 82-83
Collective unconscious, 15, 45-46
    Great Mother as reality of, 46-47
    numinous and, 15
Completeness, feminine idea of, 51
Consciousness,
    "a priori" source of, 43
    dawn of, 11
    historical, 43-44
    "indispensable place" concept of, 43
    patriarchal, 47-48, 59-61
    relationship between divine matrix and, 49
Contamination, Jung's concept of, 22
Continuity, Jung's theory of human/animal, 42-43
Creation, Jung on nature of, 18
Creative *dynamics*, 80-81

D

Date: 26-Mar-90 12:29 EST
Denifle, H. S., 76
Divine matrix,
    relation to human, 18-19
    relationship between consciousness and, 49
Divine perfection, 12-13
Divinity, 79-80
Dominicans, Eckhart and, 74-75
Dream, Jung's significant, 41-43
Dynamics (creative), 80-81

E

Eckhart, Meister, 18, 66, 70-98
    affinity of experience with Jung, 69-98
    background of, 73-76
    on birth of God, 92-93
    on gnostic thought, 78

102

The Son (logos), Jung's perception of, 20 24
Soul, Jung's perspective on the, 79-82
Stein, Murray, 96
St. George, myth of, 62-63
Suffering,
    Eckhart's perception of, 77
    of human historical consciousness, 22-23
Summa Theologica (Aquinas), 6
Suso, Heinrich, 76
Symbols of self, 95
Synchronicity, as symbol of self, 95
"Systematic blindness", 4
Systematic Theology (Tillich), 11

T

Tauler, Johann, 76
Telos (realization of self), 26
Thomism, 12
Tillich, Paul, 5, 9-12, 61
Tondi, primitive psychology of, 79
Transcendence, God and, 7
Trinitarian doctrine, 8-10
Trinitarian God, 86
Trinity, 19-23, 87-89
    Goddess as mother of, 41-68
    symbol of, 20

U

Unconscious (collective), 45-46
University of Paris, 74
Unus mundus, 95

V

Violence, Chrisitan myth and, 16-17

W

White, Victor, 33-34
Womb, reentering of, 61, 64

Y

Yaweh, 50, 52

Z

Zen tradition, 77-78, 97

STUDIES IN THE PSYCHOLOGY OF RELIGION

DATE DUE

OCT 13 1998			
DEC 2 2002			
SEP 0 8 03			

Printed in USA